# Beneath
# Surface

## Samuela Eckstut and Diana Lubelska

 LONGMAN

**Addison Wesley Longman Limited,**
*Edinburgh Gate, Harlow,*
*Essex CM20 2JE, England*
*and Associated companies throughout the world.*

© Longman Group UK Limited 1989

First published 1989
Twelfth impression 1996

Set in 9/11pt Palatino
Printed in China
SWTC/12

ISBN 0-582-79111-1

## Acknowledgements

The authors would like to thank Rena Yannopoulos, Karen Sorensen and Peter O'Leary for their help and suggestions. Special thanks also go to Kate Goldrick and Kate Lovell, and to Sheila Lambie for her encouragement and support.

The authors and publishers would like to thank all the advisers and those involved in the trialling of this material, especially the British Council Schools in Greece, Italy and Spain, and the Bell Schools in Cambridge, London and Norwich. The publishers would also like to thank all those UK schools involved in the pilot study of the Longman Skills series:

**LONDON:** International House; Central School; Davies School; Kingsway Princeton
**CAMBRIDGE:** Eurocentre; Anglo-World; Cambridge Academy
**EDINBURGH:** Stevenson College; Basil Paterson; Edinburgh Language Foundation
**EASTBOURNE:** English Centre
**TORQUAY:** Torquay International
**OXFORD:** Godmer House; Swan School; Anglo-World
**BRIGHTON:** Regent School; St Giles School
**BOURNEMOUTH:** Anglo-Continental; BEET Language Centre; English Language Centre
**HASTINGS:** International House; EF International School
**EXETER:** International School

We are grateful to the following for permission to reproduce copyright material:

The Associated Press for a simplified version of the article 'Melt fat with a fidget habit' by Daniel Q Haney from *Sunday Times Business News* 28/12/81; Jonathan Cape Ltd for the poem 'There are some men' from page 16 *The Spice Box of Earth* by Leonard Cohen (pub. Jonathan Cape Ltd); Exley Publications Ltd for extracts from *To Mum* edited by Helen and Richard Exley Copyright, © 1976 Exley Publications Ltd; The London Standard for an adapted version of the article 'Gorilla boy Levan says: I prefer monkeys' from page 3 *The London Standard* 12/9/86; Octopus Books Ltd for a slightly simplified extract from page 139 *The World's Greatest Cranks and Crackpots* by Margaret Nicholas; Sidgwick & Jackson Ltd for an adapted extract from *Is That It?* by Bob Geldof; Syndication International (1986) Ltd for simplified versions of the articles 'Half a croissant and a heat log' by

Paul Simper from pages 22–23 *No 1* magazine 25/1/86 and 'Warning! Don't Go Near The Water' by Sue Thomas from page 48 *Woman* magazine; the author, Vivien Tomlinson and The Sunday Times Magazine for an adapted version of her article 'Splitting The Image' from page 9 *The Sunday Times Magazine* 15/6/86; Usborne Publishing Ltd for extracts from pages 3, 14 *Usborne New Technology* by Lynn Myring and Maurice Kimmitt (1984), © Usborne Publishing Ltd; the author, Monica Wells for extracts from her article 'Clothes Control' from pages 68–69 *19* magazine February 1986, © Monica Wells.

*Growing Up* (page 30) by Russell Baker, pub Congdon and Weed Inc. (c/o St Martin's Press Inc. New York) 1974; *The Flying Fool* (page 34) by Josh Brooman from 'The Age of Excess', pub Longman Group UK Ltd. 1986; *Little House on the Prairie* (page 58) by Laura Ingalls Wilder, pub Methuen 1970.

We are grateful to the following for permission to reproduce illustrative material in this book:

AGE FOTOStock for page 56 (bottom centre left); BBC Hulton Picture Library for page 35 (top); British Telecom for page 38 (left); Camera Press Limited/Benoit Gysembergh for page 63 (top); The J Allan Cash Photo Library page 56 (top right, bottom centre right and bottom right); Greg Evans Photo Library for page 38 (right); Exley Publications Limited/Sean Charlton for page 11; Exley Publications Limited/Maxine Howitt for page 10; Robert Harding Picture Library for page 56 (top left); Martin and Michael Henfield for page 42 (top); Methuen and Company Limited/Garth Williams for page 58; National Westminster Bank PLC for page 50; Popperfoto for pages 35 (bottom) and 63 (bottom right); Sidgwick and Jackson for page 63 (bottom left); Solo Syndication and Literary Agency Limited for page 18 (left); Peter de Sousa for page 18 (right); Tony Stone Photo Library – London for page 56 (top centre); Sunday Times/Michael Heath for page 26; Sunday Times/Barry Lewis for page 42 (bottom); Topham Picture Library for pages 55 and 56 (bottom left); Monica Wells for pages 70 and 71.

Illustrated by Nancy Anderson, Ray Burrows, Karl Mather and Stephen Wright.

# Contents

# Map of the book

| Unit | Topic/Text type | Reading skills | Vocabulary/Grammar |
|---|---|---|---|
| 1 | Family relationships<br>Anecdotes | **Read the text:** skimming<br>**Check your understanding:**<br>1 meaning from context<br>2 complex sentences<br>3 main ideas | Collocations with *make* and *do*; embedded questions |
| 2 | Unusual people<br>Biographical account | **Read the text:** predicting<br>**Check your understanding:**<br>1 meaning from context<br>2 extracting relevant information<br>3 explicit and implicit information | Prefix *un-*; *so* + adjective + *that* |
| 3 | Animals<br>Newspaper article | **Read the text:** predicting<br>**Check your understanding:**<br>1 meaning from context<br>2 relations between parts of a text | Compound adjectives; irregular verb forms |
| 4 | Friendship<br>Poem | **Read the text:** gist<br>**Check your understanding:**<br>1 meaning from context<br>2 the main idea<br>3 implicit information | Homophones; word order – frequency adverbs |
| 5 | Dieting<br>Newspaper article | **Read the text:** scanning<br>**Check your understanding:**<br>1 meaning from context<br>2 details | Synonyms – *fat/thin*; advice using *should* |
| 6 | Fear<br>Autobiography | **Read the text:** predicting<br>**Check your understanding:**<br>1 meaning from context<br>2 relating information to a drawing | Suffix *-en*; imperatives |
| 7 | Fame<br>Biographical account | **Read the text:** scanning<br>**Check your understanding:**<br>1 meaning from context<br>2 using reference words<br>3 explicitly stated information | Prefix *re-*; adverbs as modifiers of verbs |
| 8 | Innovations<br>Advertisement | **Read the text:** predicting<br>**Check your understanding:**<br>1 using reference words<br>2 extracting relevant information<br>3 implicitly stated information | Compound nouns; *one/ones* |

| Unit | Topic/Text type | Reading skills | Vocabulary/Grammar |
|------|-----------------|----------------|--------------------|
| 9 | Twins<br>Magazine article | **Read the text:** predicting<br>**Check your understanding:**<br>1 the main idea<br>2 meaning from context<br>3 relations between parts of a text | Homonyms; *used to* + verb |
| 10 | Water safety<br>Magazine article | **Read the text:** scanning<br>**Check your understanding:**<br>1 meaning from context<br>2 transferring information to a diagram<br>3 explicit and implicit information | Derived forms; comparative and superlative forms of adjectives |
| 11 | Saving money<br>Advertisement | **Read the text:** gist<br>**Check your understanding:**<br>1 meaning from context<br>2 extracting relevant information<br>3 details<br>4 function of a text | Money; mass/count nouns |
| 12 | Personalities<br>Magazine interview | **Read the text:** gist<br>**Check your understanding:**<br>1 using reference words<br>2 meaning from context<br>3 details | Hyponomy – place; *some/any/every/no* compounds |
| 13 | Dangerous situations<br>Fiction | **Read the text:** predicting<br>**Check your understanding:**<br>1 the main idea<br>2 recognising tone<br>3 relations between parts of a text | Homonyms; past progressive |
| 14 | World hunger<br>Magazine article | **Read the text:** predicting<br>**Check your understanding:**<br>1 the main idea<br>2 meaning from context<br>3 explicit and implicit information | Suffix *-ful*; reported speech |
| 15 | Lasers<br>General<br>non-fiction | **Read the text:** predicting<br>**Check your understanding:**<br>1 recognising syntactical elements<br>2 communicative value of a sentence<br>3 note-making; extracting relevant information | Sound/spelling correspondence; defining relative clauses |
| 16 | Appearance and personality<br>Magazine article | **Read the text:** gist<br>**Check your understanding:**<br>1 communicative value of a sentence<br>2 details | Clothing; gerund as object of preposition |

# To the teacher

*Beneath the Surface* is the second in a three-book series designed to improve pre-intermediate students' reading skills in English. The texts are from a variety of authentic sources.

The book consists of sixteen units. Each unit contains pre-reading activities, comprehension exercises, discussion points, vocabulary work, grammar practice and a related writing task. Though students will meet quite complex language, the tasks they are asked to do are at their level of ability.

A removable answer key is provided for the teacher and for students using the book on their own.

It should take one class period (45–60 minutes) to do the basic cycle of work in class. The writing task may be assigned as homework. The vocabulary and grammar sections (indicated by a tint box in the margin) are outside the core lesson, and can be used as additional activities or homework. The nine sections of each unit are described below.

## WHAT ABOUT YOU?

This section includes discussion points to introduce students to the general subject of the text and to arouse their interest. The discussion points activate students' previous knowledge on the subject and relate the material to their own experience. Students should share all information with each other as the more background knowledge they possess on a subject, the more comprehensible texts will be.

In many units new vocabulary also appears in this section. Students who know the meanings of any of these words can explain them to the others. If not, the teacher will need to explain.

Students should look at this section before they see the text, and students working on their own should also consider these questions.

## BEFORE YOU READ

This section introduces students to the text. The activities use the visuals and graphics to help students learn as much as they can about the text before they actually read it. Other activities ask students to scan the text for specific information and/or to predict its contents.

## READ THE TEXT

Students are asked to read the text in order to complete a specific task. This may include skimming the text, checking the correctness of their predictions, noting feelings which the text arouses in them and other activities one normally engages in when reading a text for the first time. In this way, students always have a reason for reading the text.

## TEXT

The text appears after the pre-reading tasks. Visuals which accompanied the original text and/or aid comprehension also appear with the text.

## CHECK YOUR UNDERSTANDING

These exercises are designed to *teach* comprehension *not* to test it. They draw attention to the writer's main points, help students understand difficult areas of a text, and give them practice in skills that they can transfer to their reading outside of the classroom.

Some of the skills dealt with in this section include:
- guessing meaning from context
- understanding explicitly stated information
- understanding implicitly stated information
- understanding details
- understanding the main idea
- understanding relations between parts of a text

## WHAT DO YOU THINK?

Students relate what they have read to their own experience. They should discuss their feelings about what they have read and the implications of points raised by the writer. To maximise student talking time this section should be done in pairs or groups while the teacher moves from group to group 'eavesdropping' on what the students are saying.

## VOCABULARY FOCUS

This section takes students beyond the reading lesson and allows them to work on extending their vocabulary in a specific lexical area. The exercises in this section are based on one or more lexical items which appear in the text. They recycle and practise vocabulary in contexts outside the text and help students build up their vocabulary through word study. Exercises include areas such as prefixes and suffixes, homonyms, collocation, lexical sets, sound-spelling correspondence, word appropriacy and word derivation.

## GRAMMAR FOCUS

Like 'Vocabulary focus', this section moves on from the reading lesson and focuses students' attention on a particular structure which occurs in the text. Structures chosen normally occur in course material at this level and/or are problematical for students.

## WRITING TASK

The writing tasks are designed to extend the topic of the unit rather than to practise specific vocabulary or structures. Some tasks ask the students to respond to or summarise what they have read. Others ask students to write a description or instructions for a subject related to that of the text. By finishing the unit with a written task, students have the opportunity to consolidate what they have learnt.

# To the student

*Beneath The Surface* is designed to help pre-intermediate students read better in English. There are sixteen texts taken from a variety of newspapers, magazines and books. These texts have been chosen because they are interesting, informative and/or amusing. The exercises before and after each text will help you understand what you have read.

   The texts at the beginning of the book are easier than those at the end. Therefore, if you wish, you can start with Unit One and work through the units in order.

   None of the texts you are going to read has been written for students of English, so there will be many unknown words. Sometimes you will be asked to guess what some of these words mean. Other times there are definitions for a few words at the end of the text. However, there will always be words which you do not know. Do not worry about these words. You do not need to understand every word in order to understand the information in the text.

   If you are using this book on your own, there is a removable key for the exercises in each unit which have the symbol K . Most of the exercises in the 'What about you' and 'What do you think' sections are for discussion. You will see the symbol next to them. Do not ignore these exercises. Think about the answers, and if you like, write them down. It will help you understand the text.

# To Mum

**What about you?**

1 What does your mother (or another close female relative) look like?
2 How old is she?
3 Does she work outside the home? What does she do?
4 Which of these words describe her?

beautiful ☐        hard-working ☐        kind ☐        tall ☐

friendly ☐        helpful ☐        nervous ☐        thin ☐

funny ☐        interesting ☐        quiet ☐        young ☐

5 What other words would you use to describe your mother?

**Before you read**

You are going to read nine extracts from a book called *To Mum*. In this book children between the ages of ten and sixteen talk about their mothers. Put a tick (✓) next to the sentence(s) which you think are true.

1 They are going to say nice things about their mothers. ☐

2 They are going to say funny things about their mothers. ☐

3 They are going to talk about the strange things mothers say and do. ☐

**Read the text**

Read the extracts. Put a tick (✓) next to those which you think are funny.

When I ask Mum how old she is she always says twenty-one. As I have a sister who is twenty-two even dumb old me knows this cannot be right.
Billy Mayhook (Age 13) ☐

Mums are the sort of people who, before a film starts in the evening, send you to bed saying how awful it will be and then wake you up saying what a fantastic film it was.
Nicholas (Age 11) ☐

I have a super mother who makes cakes, puts them in the pantry and doesn't notice when I eat them.
Mark Wickham-Jones (Age 13) ☐

My Mum Christmas shopping

My mum says I'm nicest when I'm asleep because I can not say anything wrong.
Richard (Age 12) ☐

My mum she works so very hard,
She must be near to tears,
Cos' gimie, gimie[1]!   More, More!
Are the only words she hears.

She only wants the magic word,
Oh by the way it's PLEASE
She acts just like a servant,
But never asks for fees.

Susan Harris
(Age 10)

Mothers do not die because they live in the hearts of their children.
Berna Tahmiscioglu
(Age 16)

The way my mum worries at exam time anyone would think she was taking them not me.
Robert Booth
(Age 13)

My mum is going to have a baby and she told me that she can't smack me till after April.
Simon
(Age 10)

My mum says' Yes dear' when she does not know what I'm talking about.
Tanya
(Age 10)

[1]Cos' gimie, gimie: Because give me, give me

**Check your understanding**

*1* Find the words in the extracts which have the same meanings as the words in Column A. Write these words in the blanks.

| COLUMN A | COLUMN B | | COLUMN A | COLUMN B | |
|---|---|---|---|---|---|
| 1 not clever | (Billy) | _____ | 4 very good | (Nicholas) | _____ |
| 2 hit | (Simon) | _____ | 5 very good | (Mark) | _____ |
| 3 very bad | (Nicholas) | _____ | 6 see | (Mark) | _____ |

*2* Read what Billy, Robert and Nicholas said again. The sentences below say the same thing but use different words. Fill in the blanks with the correct words.

1 'Mum, _____ _____ are you?' I often ask my mother. '_____ _____ ' she says. This _____ _____ correct because my sister is _____ _____ .

2 When I take my _____ , my mother _____ a lot. This is very strange because she is not _____ _____ . I am taking them.

3 Even if there is a film on TV in the evening, you still must go to _____ . Mothers don't want you to feel bad so they say, 'The film will be _____ .' But when they wake you up in the morning, they say, 'The film was _____ .'

11

*3* Imagine that the children's mothers have written about their children. Match the mothers' comments with the names of the children. Write down the names of the children in the blanks. Look at number 2 as an example. (Be careful! One mother's comment is missing.)

1 'I want my son to be a good student.'     _____

2 'My son is lucky. I can't smack him these days.'     *Simon*

3 'I never tell people my real age.'     _____

4 'My daughter thinks that I don't hear what she says.'     _____

5 'My son always says the wrong thing at the wrong time.'     _____

6 'I would like somebody to help me in the house.'     _____

7 'My son always wants to watch films that are on late at night.'     _____

8 'My son loves my food.'     _____

**What do you think?**

1 Do any of the extracts describe your mother or another relative of yours? Which one(s)?

2 Think about when you were small. What event do you remember well about you and your mother or you and another relative?

**Vocabulary focus**

> My mother **makes** cakes.      My mother sometimes **does** strange things.

*1* Look at the words below. Write them in the columns under the correct verb. Look at the examples.

dinner            housework
exercises       a mistake
(someone) a favour    money
a good job       a paper aeroplane
homework       a promise

| MAKE | DO |
|---|---|
| *a promise* | *(someone) a favour* |

*2* Use your own ideas to fill in the blanks with the words from Exercise 1. If you wish, you can use the same words twice.

1 I hate doing _____ .      5 I hate making _____ .

2 I love doing _____ .      6 I love making _____ .

3 Will you do _____ ?      7 Will you make _____ ?

4 I never do _____ .      8 I never make _____ .

| When I ask how old **she is** she always says twenty-one. |
| --- |

Look at the different word order in the sentence above and in this question:
   How old *is she*?
In the question the <u>verb</u> comes <u>before</u> *she*. In the sentence the <u>verb</u> comes <u>after</u> *she*.

*1* Put these words in the correct order.

1 where/lives/do/she/you/know    _____ ?

2 was/asked/late/her/I/why/she    _____ .

3 happened/I/how/don't/it/know    _____ .

4 costs/she/it/much/know/how/does    _____ ?

*2* Put a tick (✓) next to the sentences which are correct. Put a cross (✗) next to the sentences which are wrong and correct them. Look at questions 1 and 2 as examples.

1 Please tell me where he lives.   I bought   ☑

2 Do you want to know what ~~did I buy?~~   ☒

3 Ask her how much this does cost.   ☐

4 Do you know what time is it?   ☐

5 He doesn't know where she went.   ☐

6 I'd like to know why is Barbara unhappy.   ☐

7 Can you tell me where I can get some water? ☐

Imagine that the authors of *To Mum* have asked you to write about your mother or another relative. You can say what she (or he) looks like and what she (or he) is like as a person. Begin like this:

   My _____ is a very special person. She (*or* He). . .

# Linen Cook

**What about you?**

1  Put a tick ( ✓ ) if you think these people have strange habits.

☐ a) Mr Chambers has a dog. The dog eats with him, sleeps in his bed, goes to work with him and goes on holiday with him.

☐ b) Lilly always has hot milk and rice before she goes to bed and when she wakes up.

☐ c) Morris always wears a hat when he sleeps.

☐ d) Mrs Melville eats only fruit, nuts and vegetables.

2  Do you know anybody with a strange habit? What do they do that is strange?

**Before you read**

You are going to read a text called *White for all occasions*. Below is a list of words from the text. Discuss with another student or write down what you think the text is about.

| | | | |
|---|---|---|---|
| 17th-century | suits, coats and hats | farm | white |
| Robert Cook | famous | horses | eighty years old |

_____

_____

**Read the text**

Read the text. Did you guess what the text was about?

WHITE   FOR   ALL   OCCASIONS

# LINEN COOK

THE HUMANE[1] HEALTH ADDICT

The 17th-century Irish farmer Robert Cook was the most unusual figure in County Waterford. He always wore white linen. His underwear, night clothes and shirts were in purest white, and so were his suits, coats and hats. He became so famous for his clothes and his passion for
5  white that he was known all over Ireland as 'Linen Cook'.

He refused to have any brown cows in the field of his farm at Cappoquin and even his horses had to be the same pure white as his clothes.

Cook was a passionate vegetarian and refused to eat the flesh of any
10  animal or to wear anything produced by an animal.

A fox which attacked his chickens was not killed when it was caught. Instead, he gave it a lecture on the evils of murder, then offered it a sporting chance by making it run through a line of his farm workers, who had sticks.[2]
15  Cook had a long and healthy life and showed that 'water for drink, vegetables for food and linen and other plant life for clothing were enough to live on'.

He died in 1726 when he was over eighty years old and was buried in a white linen shroud[3].

[1]*humane*: kind to animals and other people
[2]*sticks*: long thin pieces of wood
[3]*shroud*: the cloth for covering a dead body at burial

**Check your understanding**

*K*

**1** Put a circle around the correct answer.

1 *Linen* (*line 2*) is a kind of
   a) food
   b) animal
   c) cloth

2 *Passion* (*line 4*) means
   a) a strong feeling
   b) a serious problem
   c) fear

3 *Refused* (*line 6*) means
   a) didn't love
   b) didn't do
   c) didn't know

4 *Vegetarians* (*line 9*) are people who do not
   a) eat animals
   b) buy animals
   c) kill animals

5 *Attacked* (*line 11*) means tried to
   a) kill
   b) see
   c) find

6 *Lecture* (*line 12*) means
   a) a lot of food
   b) a little water
   c) a long talk

7 *Evils* (*line 12*) means something
   a) important
   b) good
   c) bad

8 *Buried* (*line 18*) means
   a) put a dead person in the ground
   b) killed someone
   c) gave someone clothes to wear

**2** Fill in the information about the subject of the text. Look at the example.

Name: Robert Cook     Other name: _____

Country: _____     Occupation: _____

Year of death: _____

What he preferred:

   Clothes: _____     Food: _____

   Horses: _____     Drink: _____

**3** What do you learn about Robert Cook from the text. Put a tick ( ✓) next to the correct statements.

1 He didn't think people should kill animals. ☐

2 He didn't wear leather shoes or woollen clothes. ☐

3 He never ate meat. ☐

4 He was married. ☐

5 He didn't like the colour brown. ☐

**What do you think?**

1 Why do you think Robert Cook wanted everything to be white?
2 A health addict always worries about his or her health. Why does the writer call Robert Cook a health addict?
3 In what ways was Robert Cook humane?
4 Are you wearing anything that Robert Cook wouldn't wear? Have you eaten anything today that he wouldn't eat?
5 Are you a vegetarian? Do you know any vegetarians? Why do people become vegetarians?
6 If Robert Cook were alive today, what would he not like about modern life?

**Vocabulary focus**

> Robert Cook was the most **unusual** figure in County Waterford.

The prefix *un-* often means *not*: *un + usual = not usual*

*1* Write down the meanings of the words below.

1 unlucky _____

2 unimportant _____

3 unnecessary _____

4 unable _____

*2* Below are four more words which begin with *un-*. However, the letters are not in the correct order. Put the letters in the correct order and write the words in the blanks. Look at number 1 as an example.

1 tanpelsanu __unpleasant__

2 indunk _____

3 puynaph _____

4 hulaythen _____

*3* Fill in each blank with one word from Exercises 2 and 3.

1 I'm afraid I was _____ to do my homework because I was busy.

2 In many countries people think that the number thirteen and black cats are

_____ .

3 He was very _____ after the test because he didn't do well.

4 Eating a lot of sweets and ice cream is _____ .

5 It was _____ for you to come. We have finished all the work.

> Robert Cook became **so** famous for his clothes and his passion for white **that** he was known all over Ireland as 'Linen Cook'.

We use *so + adjective + that* to talk about *results*.

**1** Make sentences with *so . . . that* by matching Columns A and B. Write the correct letter from Column B in each box.

| COLUMN *A* | COLUMN *B* |
|---|---|
| 1 I'm so ill ☐ | a) that I didn't buy anything. |
| 2 The music was so loud ☐ | b) that I could drink a whole bottle of water. |
| .3 Your letters are so small ☐ | c) that I can't move. |
| 4 The clothes were so expensive ☐ | d) that I couldn't hear you. |
| 5 I'm so thirsty ☐ | e) that I can't read what you have written. |

**2** Complete the sentences using your own ideas.

1 It's so hot that _____ .

2 I'm so tired that _____ .

3 The film was so good that _____ .

4 My holiday was so wonderful that _____ .

**Writing task**

If you know somebody who has some unusual habits, write a description of this person. In your description say:
- who this person is
- how you know him or her
- what his or her unusual habits are
- why you think he or she has these habits

If you do not know anybody, write a description of an imaginary person with unusual habits.
Begin like this:
I know a person with some rather unusual habits. His (*or* Her) name is _____ , and he (*or* she) . . .

# Gorilla Boy Levan

**What about you?**

1 When was the last time you went to a zoo? Do you remember anything special about that last visit?
2 In what ways can going to the zoo be dangerous?
3 What is your favourite animal at the zoo?
4 Which animal do you think is the most frightening?

**Before you read**

Look at the pictures which accompany this unit's reading. Below are ten words and phrases in the order in which they appear in the text. Write down or tell another student what you think the article is about.

| | | |
|---|---|---|
| little boy | fell | visit him again |
| gorillas | keep him warm | nice |
| accident | a broken arm | |
| zoo | remembers | |

_____

_____

**Read the text**

Read the article. Did you predict what the story was about?

# Gorilla boy Levan says: I prefer monkeys

## FIVE-YEAR-OLD LEAVES HOSPITAL
by Lynda Murdin

The little boy who changed the public image of gorillas faced the cameras today for the first time since his accident and declared: 'I
5 still like zoos – but not gorillas. I like monkeys.'

Levan Merritt, five, fell into the gorilla pit at Jersey Zoo on the first day of a family holiday last month
10 and his parents held their breath as the seven-foot[1] tall eighteen-stone[2] Jambo approached him.

The gentle giant bent over and stroked[3] the little boy and adjusted
15 his clothing to keep him warm.

Levan was flown to Southampton Hospital with a fractured skull[4], a panda-sized black eye and a broken arm.
20 His father, Steve, a thirty-four-

[1]_seven foot_: 2.10 metres
[2]_eighteen-stone_: about 115 kilograms
[3]_stroked_: touched nicely
[4]_a fractured skull_: a head injury

18

year-old heating engineer, said: 'We want to take him back to the zoo so that he doesn't lose his love for animals.'

25     His mother, Pauline, twenty-eight, said: 'He has no more nightmares about the gorilla standing over him.

30    'He has told the doctors he fell in with the monkeys and he thinks he remembers a bit about it, but does not talk about it.'

Levan, who has a cat called Kitkins and a hamster[5] called 35 Tommy, said: 'I don't remember falling or going to the zoo. The gorilla's name is Jambo, but I am not going to visit him again.'

And he shook his head[6] when 40 asked if he knew the gorilla had been nice to him.

Levan, surrounded by get well cards and presents, said: 'I'm better now, thank you.'

[5]*hamster*

[6]*shook his head*: said 'no' by moving his head

**Check your understanding**

*1* Write the correct answer to each question in the blank and guess the meaning of the words and phrases in *italics*.

1 Were Levan's parents worried when the gorilla went near him?    _____

Did they know what the gorilla would do?    _____

Did they wait to see what would happen?    _____

So, what does *held their breath* (*line 10*) mean?

a) They waited with worry. ☐

b) They stopped breathing. ☐

2 Did the gorilla go near the boy or walk away from him?    _____

So, what does *approached* (*line 12*) mean? _____

3 Was the gorilla nice to the boy?    _____

Did the gorilla touch the boy lightly, or did he hit him?    _____

So, what does *gentle* (*line 13*) mean?

a) bad ☐

b) kind ☐

4 Did the gorilla take off the boy's clothes?    _____

Did the gorilla have other clothes for the boy in the pit?    _____

Did he move the clothes that the boy was wearing a little?    _____

So, what does *adjusted* (*line 14*) mean? _____

5 After the accident, did the boy have good or bad dreams?    _____

So, what does *nightmares* (*line 27*) mean? _____

6 What does *pit* (*line 8*) mean? _____

7 What does *surrounded by get well cards and presents* (*lines 42 and 43*) mean? _____

**2** Below are four other paragraphs which appeared in the article. Read them and then answer the questions. Write the letter of the correct paragraph in each box.

[1]*skin graft*: taking a piece of healthy skin and putting it on another part of the body which has been damaged

a) He will probably go home to Horsham, Sussex this weekend for a few days before returning to the hospital for a skin graft[1].

b) And his mother added: 'We are just glad he's all right, because we blame ourselves.'

c) The dramatic moment was filmed by an amateur video cameraman and the film thrilled the world.

d) 'Although he has seen the video, he doesn't associate himself with the boy lying there.'

1 Which paragraph should be between paragraphs 3 and 4 of the article? ☐

2 Which paragraph should be between paragraphs 4 and 5 of the article? ☐

3 Which paragraph should be between paragraphs 6 and 7 of the article? ☐

4 Which paragraph should be at the end of the article? ☐

## What do you think?

1 How do you think the boy fell into the gorilla pit?
2 How do you explain the gorilla's behaviour? Do you think Jambo is typical of gorillas? Why?/Why not?
3 Have you ever heard of a similar accident? What happened to the person?
4 What do you think you would do if you found yourself near a gorilla?

## Vocabulary focus

> a **thirty-four-year-old** engineer

Look at this:
A child who is *five years old* is a *five-year-old* child. (NOT a *five-years-old* child)

**1** Fill in each blank with the correct adjective form. Look at number 1 as an example.

1 The engineer is thirty-four years old.
   He is a __thirty-four-year-old__ engineer.

2 The flight lasted four hours.           It was a _____ flight.
3 Our baby is six months old.             We have a _____ baby.
4 We walked five miles.                   We had a _____ walk.
5 The chicken I bought weighed two kilos. I bought a _____ chicken.
6 Have you got ten pounds?                Have you got a _____ note?

His parents **held** their breath.    He **shook** his head.

**1** Find the twelve verbs and their past tense and past participle forms in the box.
Put a circle around each of them. (If the past and past participle forms are the
same, they appear only once in the box.) Look at the examples. (Hint: You will
find one form of each of the verbs in the text on pages 18–19.)

| | | | | | | | | | | | | |
|---|---|---|---|---|---|---|---|---|---|---|---|---|
| b | t | h | o | u | g | h | t | x | b | t | g | i | a |
| e | a | b | s | h | a | k | e | s | h | a | k | e | n |
| n | k | n | o | w | f | e | l | l | l | k | v | f | w |
| d | e | m | q | f | l | y | l | o | s | e | r | a | c |
| y | n | u | e | t | e | f | h | k | b | e | p | l | v |
| s | s | k | n | o | w | n | r | k | e | p | t | l | t |
| f | a | l | l | o | q | h | l | n | n | h | h | e | w |
| s | h | o | o | k | o | o | p | e | t | e | i | n | d |
| a | t | p | s | j | f | l | o | w | n | l | n | m | a |
| y | y | k | t | o | l | d | s | a | i | d | k | e | i |

**2** Write all the verb forms you have found in the correct column.

*VERB*          *PAST*          *PAST PARTICIPLE*

1 _____        _____        _____
2 _____        _____        _____
3 _____        _____        _____
4 _____        _____        _____
5 _____        _____        _____
6 _____        _____        _____
7 _____        _____        _____
8 _____        _____        _____
9 _____        _____        _____
10 _____       _____        _____
11 _____       _____        _____
12 _____       _____        _____

**Writing task**

Write a description of what you think happened the next time Levan Merritt
went to the zoo. Say:
 • how long after his accident he went to the zoo
 • if he went to see the gorillas
 • what he did at the zoo
 • how he felt while he was there

# There Are Some Men

**What about you?**

1 How often do you read a poem? Do you like reading poems? Why? Why not?
2 Whom are you named after?
3 What two adjectives would you use to describe a mountain?
4 Are any mountains in your country named after people? If so, which one(s)?

**Before you read**

1 What is the poem called?
2 Who is it by?
3 When was the poet born?
4 How many verses are there in the poem?
5 How many sentences are in each verse?

**Read the text**

Read the poem. What is it about?

---

### THERE ARE SOME MEN

There are some men
who should have mountains
to bear their names to time[1].

Grave-markers are not high enough
5  or green,
and sons go far away
to lose the fist
their father's hand will always seem.

I had a friend:
10  he lived and died in mighty silence
and with dignity[2],
left no book, son, or lover to mourn.

Nor is this a mourning-song
but only a naming of this mountain
15  on which I walk,
fragrant, dark, and softly white
under the pale of mist[3].
I name this mountain after him.

Leonard Cohen
Canadian poet, 1934-

---

[1]*to bear their names to time*: to remember them forever
[2]*dignity*: serious and calm behaviour
[3]*under the pale of mist*: in an area covered with thin fog

**Check your understanding**

K

**1** The sentences below explain in part the meaning of the words in *italics*. Read the poem again. Then choose the correct word from the list below to complete the meaning. Write one word in each blank. (Note: You will not be able to use all of the words.)

also      closed    not    stayed
angry    died       sad    sweet

1 A *grave-marker* (*line 4*) is usually a piece of stone which says the name of a person, when this person was born and when he or she _____ .

2 A *fist* (*line 7*) is the shape of the hand when the fingers are _____ .

3 Someone *left* (*line 12*) the child. The person went away but the child

_____ .

4 People *mourn* (*line 12*) after someone has died. They feel very _____ and often show these feelings.

5 *Nor is this a mourning-song* (*line 13*) means the same as this is _____ a mourning song.

6 If something is *fragrant* (*line 16*), it smells _____ .

**2** What is the main idea of each verse? Write the correct letter in each box.

|c| Verse 1      a) The poet says what happened to a friend of his.

|d| Verse 2      b) The poet says why he is writing the poem.

|a| Verse 3      c) The poet says that we should remember some people forever.

|b| Verse 4      d) The poet says why giving someone's name to a mountain will help us remember this person forever.

**3** The poet gives several reasons for choosing a mountain (rather than, for example, a river or a street) to name his friend after. What reason does he give in each of the phrases below? Put a tick ( ✓ ) in the correct box. Look at number 1 as an example.

|  | Mountains are always there | People can see mountains from far away | Mountains are beautiful |
|---|---|---|---|
| 1 to time | ✓ | | |
| 2 Grave-markers are not high enough | | ✓ | |
| 3 (Grave markers are not) green | | | ✓ |
| 4 sons go far away | ✓ | | |
| 5 fragrant, dark and softly white | | | ✓ |

**What do you think?**

1  Why do you think the poet's friend was so important to him? Or, does the poet feel the same way about all his friends?
2  Do you think the poet's friend was a famous person? Why?/Why not?
3  Do you think he is talking about a) a friend b) men c) men and women?
4  What tense is used in each verse? Why is there this change?
5  What picture do you see when you read the poem? How does it make you feel?

**Vocabulary focus**

> Nor is this a **mourning** song

Many words in English sound the same but have a different spelling and meaning. For example, *mourning* sounds the same as *morning* but has a different spelling and meaning.

*1* The words missing in each pair of sentences sound the same but have a different spelling and meaning. Fill in each blank with the correct words. Look at number 1 as an example.

1  a) We went swimming in the ___**sea**___ .
   b) I can't ___**see**___ what the sign says. Can you?
2  a) People ___hear___ with their ears.
   b) The book isn't ___here___ . Where is it?
3  a) I want to ___write___ a letter. Have you got a pen?
   b) When you get to Hill Road, turn ___right___ .
4  a) I ___knew___ all the answers on the test. I was very happy.
   b) Have you seen my ___new___ watch? I bought it yesterday.
5  a) Some mountains are not ___high___ enough.
   b) ___Hi___ , Barbara. How are you?

*2* In Column B write the word which sounds like the word in Column A. Then write down the meaning of this word or give an example of how it is used. Look at number 1 as an example.

COLUMN *A*

1  *mourning*
   • what people often do after someone dies
2  *peace*
   • when there is no war
3  *brake*
   • when you want to stop a car or bicycle
4  *aloud*
   • people hear you when you read like this
5  *deer*
   • this is an animal
6  *weigh*
   • you do this to find out how many kilos you are

COLUMN *B*

**morning**
**the early part of the day**
_____
_____
_____
_____
_____
_____
_____
_____
_____
_____

their father's hand **will always seem**

*1* The sentences below explain in part the meaning of the words in *italics*. Read the poem again. Then choose the correct word from the list below to complete the meaning. Write one word in each blank. (Note: You will not be able to use all of the words.)

*Examples:*

1 She *always* leaves at 8:00.
2 I *never* understand what he says.
3 I'm *sometimes* ill after a heavy meal.
4 I was *rarely* tired at my old job.
5 Do they *usually* come late?
6 She doesn't *often* work at night.

*THE RULES*

1 When the verb has one part (sentences 1 and 2), where do we put the adverb?
_____ the verb.

2 When the verb is *am, is* or *are* (sentence 3), where do we put the adverb?
_____ the verb.

3 When the verb is *was* or *were* (sentence 4), where do we put the adverb?
_____ the verb.

4 When the verb has two parts (sentences 5 and 6), where do we put the adverb?
_____ the second verb.

5 Which other adverbs have the same position as *always* (all the sentences)?

_____ , _____ , _____ , _____ , _____

*2* Read the sentences below. Put a tick ( ✓) if the sentence is correct. Put a cross (✕) if the sentence is wrong. Then correct the wrong sentences. Look at number 1 as an example.

1 I never am tired after I swim.  ☒  *I am never tired*

2 Do you often see your neighbours?  ☐  _____

3 Rarely Christopher eats meat.  ☐  _____

4 She was always a good student.  ☐  _____

5 Have always you lived there?  ☐  _____

6 They have sometimes pizza for dinner. ☐  _____

**Writing task**

Imagine that you knew the poet and his friend. Write a paragraph about their friendship. Say:
- what the friend's name was
- how long they knew each other
- where they met
- the sort of things they did together
- why they were such good friends
- how the poet felt when his friend died and what he did

<table>
<tr><td>UNIT 5</td><td># Lose Fat with a Fidget Habit</td></tr>
</table>

## UNIT 5 — Lose Fat with a Fidget Habit

**What about you?**

1 Have you ever tried to lose weight? What sort of diet did you go on?
2 Put a tick ( ✓ ) next to the best way to lose weight.

☐ Eat small amounts for breakfast, lunch and dinner so that you have only 1,200 calories[1] a day.

☐ Eat only meat and vegetables.

☑ Do not eat any sweets.

☐ Take a lot of exercise (jogging, for example) so that you burn up calories.

> [1]*calorie*: a measure used for the amount of energy which a food will produce

**Before you read**

Look at the cartoon which accompanies this unit's reading and answer the questions below. Write your answers in the blanks.

1 What one word best describes the people? _____Fat_____
2 What are they doing with their fingers? _____typeng_____
3 What is the name of the class they are at? _____keep F c_____
4 Why do you think they are at the class? _____lose weight_____

**Read the text**

Read the definitions below. Then read the article and find the one word which refers to all of these actions. Write this word and an explanation of its meaning in the blanks. (Hint: There is an explanation of it in the fourth paragraph.)

General word: _____     Explanation: _____

1 *scratch*: to move your nails against a part of your body
2 *twitch*: to move suddenly and quickly when you don't want to
3 *squirm*: to continuously turn your body when nervous
4 *wiggle*: to move in small movements, especially from side to side
5 *toe-tapping*: moving the front part of your foot up and down
6 *finger-drumming*: hitting your fingers continuously and lightly against something hard

KEEP FIDGETING CLASSES

HEATH

> [1]*respiratory*: connected with breathing

# LOSE FAT WITH A FIDGET HABIT

Have you eaten too much over the holidays? You should try fidgeting for a while. Those around you might not like it, but scratching and twitching is an important way of burning up calories.

American researchers have found that some people's squirming
5 and wiggling equals several miles of jogging each day.

The scientists, based at the National Institute of Health's laboratory in Phoenix, Arizona, are studying why some people get fat and others stay slim.

In one study 177 people each spent 24 hours in the institute's
10 respiratory[1] chamber – a room where the amount of energy people expend is measured by their oxygen and carbon dioxide levels. By the end of the day, some people had burned up 800 calories in toe-tapping, finger-drumming and other nervous habits. However, others had expended only 100 calories.

15 The researchers found that slim women fidget more than fat women, but there was no significant difference in men. Heavy people expend more energy when they fidget than do thin people.

*1* Write down the words from the text which are similar in meaning to the following words. Look at the paragraph in brackets to help you.

1 but (*line 2*) _____ (*paragraph 4*)

2 important (*line 3*) _____ (*paragraph 5*)

3 burn up (*lines 3 and 12*) _____ (*paragraph 5*)

4 scientists (*line 6*) _____ (*paragraph 2*)

5 fat (*line 8*) _____ (*paragraph 5*)

6 thin (*line 17*) _____ (*paragraph 3*)

*2* Write equals (=), more than (>), or less than (<) in the boxes. Look at number 1 as an example.

1 Some people's fidgeting       = Several miles of jogging

2 Some people's fidgeting       = 800 calories

3 Some people's fidgeting       < 100 calories

4 Slim women fidget       > Fat women fidget

5 Slim men fidget       = Fat men fidget

6 The energy expended by thin people when they fidget       ☐ The energy expended by fat people when they fidget

1 Put a tick ( √ ) next to the statements which you think are true.

☐ a) Heavy people always eat more than thin people.

☐ b) Heavy people eat more often during the day than thin people.

☐ c) Thin people take more exercise than heavy people.

2 Why do you think some people get fat and other people stay slim?

3 Do you fidget a lot? What do you do when you are bored or nervous?

4 Do you think the information in this article is important or interesting? Would you tell a friend who wanted to lose weight about this article?

5 Do you think this type of research is important?

> Scientists are studying why some people get **fat** and others stay **slim**.

*1* Put the words below in the correct circle. Use your dictionary for any words which you do not know.

slim    obese    skinny    overweight

heavy    plump    slender    underweight

THIN          FAT

**2** Read the description below of the differences in meaning between the words in the list in exercise 1. Then write each word in the correct blank on the line below. Look at the two words on the line as examples.

> **Thin** is a general word to describe people who have little or no fat on their bodies. If someone is thin in a pleasant way, we say they are **slim** or (less common) **slender**, but if they are too thin they are **skinny** (informal) or **underweight.**
> *Example*  I would like to be as **slim** as you.
> She looks very **thin/skinny/underweight** after her illness.
> The opposite of thin is **fat**, but this is not very polite. **Plump, heavy** and **overweight** are all more polite ways of saying the same thing. A person who is very fat is **obese**.

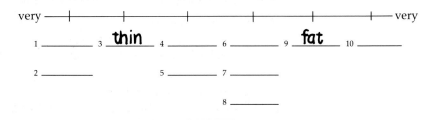

very ————|————|————|————|————|————|—— very

1 _____  3 **thin**  4 _____  6 _____  9 **fat**  10 _____

2 _____  5 _____  7 _____

8 _____

**Grammar focus**

> You **should** try fidgeting for a while.

We use *should* and *shouldn't* to give advice.

**k**  **1** Mr Hopper has tried to lose weight, but he can't. Give him some advice. Look at numbers 1 and 2 as examples.

> What am I doing wrong? I eat only one meal a day. I never eat until late at night. I take exercise at least two times a month. I eat only meat and eggs. I have sugar only when I drink coffee. I eat only two or three biscuits a day. I don't eat fruit because I know that too much sugar isn't good.

1 **You should eat three meals a day.**
2 **You shouldn't eat late at night.**
3 _____
4 _____

5 _____
6 _____
7 _____

**2** Do you have a problem at school, at work or at home? Give yourself some advice using *should* or *shouldn't*.

1 I _____

2 I _____

3 I _____

**Writing task**

Imagine that you were one of the 177 people in the fidgeting study. Write about your day at the National Institute of Health. Say:

- what time the experiment began
- what the scientists asked you to do
- if you had anything to eat while you were there
- if the scientists asked you any questions
- what time the experiment finished
- what you did when the experiment finished

Begin like this:

My day at the institute was very ⎰ boring.
⎱ strange.
  interesting.

You may want to use some of these words:

First      Then         Afterwards          Finally
Next       After that   A few (hours) later  Near the end

# Growing Up

**What about you?**

1 Can you swim? How old were you when you learned?

2 Did you take swimming lessons? If you did, what do you remember about them?

3 Which do you think is more difficult – learning how to swim when you are six, or learning to swim when you are twenty-one? Why?

**Before you read**

You are going to read an excerpt from an autobiography called *Growing Up*. In this extract the author, Russell Baker, talks about learning to swim when he was in the navy. Tick ( √) the following statements which you think will be true.

1 The swimming instructor was very helpful.  ☐

2 The writer was very afraid.  ☐

3 He learned how to swim in his first lesson.  ☐

4 The swimming instructor taught him in shallow water.  ☐

¹*20 feet = about 6½ metres*

5 At his first lesson he had to jump off a board that was more than 20 feet¹ high.  ☐

**Read the text**  *K*

Read the text. Did you tick the correct boxes?

¹*a bullhorn:*

²*line (American English): queue (British English)*

³*introduce oneself: give one's name when meeting someone for the first time*

⁴*I'm not kidding. I can't swim a stroke:* I'm serious. I can't swim at all

⁵*lifesaving equipment:*

⁶*quaking in every fiber:* shaking a lot from fear

⁷*unable to faint:* he wanted to become weak and fall but he couldn't

⁸*The impact . . . two-by-four:* hitting the water felt like someone had hit me with a piece of wood

Learning to swim had been surprisingly easy, thanks to the Navy's policy of dealing with fear by ignoring it. My fear of deep water left the Navy simply uninterested. On the first day in the pool an instructor with a voice like a bullhorn¹ ordered fifty of us to climb a high board and jump

5 in feet first. The board looked about two hundred feet high, though it may have been only twenty or twenty-five. A line² was formed to mount the ladder and jump. I drifted to the end of the line, then stepped out when the splashing started and introduced myself³ to the instructor.

'I'm a nonswimmer,' I said. 'You want me to go to the shallow end of

10 the pool?' At City College I'd spent four years in the shallow end of the pool.

'This pool doesn't have a shallow end,' the instructor said.

'Well, what am I going to do?'

'Get up on that platform and jump,' he said.

15 The pool depth was marked as fifteen feet at that point.

'I'm not kidding. I can't swim a stroke⁴.'

'Up! Up!' he shouted.

'But I'll drown.'

'This pool's got the best lifesaving equipment⁵ in the Navy,' he said.

20 'Don't worry about it.'

'Come on.'

'I'm giving you an order, mister. Up!'

Quaking in every fiber⁶, I climbed the ladder, edged out onto the board, took one look down, and, unable to faint⁷, stepped back.

25 'Jump!' the instructor roared.

I stepped to the edge, closed my eyes, and walked into space. The impact of the water was like being smacked on the bottom by a two-by-four⁸, then I was sinking, then . . . my God! . . . I was rising irresistibly to the surface. My head broke water. The water was actually supporting

30 me, just as everybody had always said it would. The instructor glared.

'You didn't keep your legs straight,' he shouted. 'Get back up there and do it again.'

**Check your understanding**

*k*

**1** Match the words in Column A with their meanings in Column B. Write the correct letter from Column B in each box. (Be careful! There are two extra choices.)

COLUMN **A**

1 thanks to (*line 1*)

2 ignore (*line 2*)

3 though (*line 5*)

4 mount (*line 6*)

5 drift (*line 7*)

6 step (*lines 7, 24 and 26*)

7 roar (*line 25*)

8 surface (*line 29*)

9 support (*line 29*)

10 glare (*line 30*)

COLUMN **B**

☐ a)  to not pay attention to someone's problems

☐ b)  to look at someone angrily

☐ c)  in addition to

☐ d)  to say very loudly

☐ e)  but

☐ f)  the top part of the water

☐ g)  to be very afraid

☐ h)  to climb

☐ i)  because of

☐ j)  to stop from going down in the water

  k)  to move slowly

  l)  to walk a short distance

**2** There are eight mistakes in the pictures below. Put a circle around each of the mistakes. Then correct them. Look at the example.

31

**What do you think?**

1 How do you think the writer felt when the instructor ordered him to jump again? What do you think he did?
2 The writer did not know how to swim. Do you think the instructor was right when he made the writer jump into deep water? Why/Why not?
3 What opinion do you think the other people at the pool had of Russell Baker?
4 Would you like to read more of *Growing Up*? Why?/Why not?

**Vocabulary focus**

| My fear of **deep** water | The pool **depth** |
|---|---|

*1* Write down the adjective form of the words below. Look at number 1 as an example.

| NOUN | ADJECTIVE |
|---|---|
| 1 depth | deep |
| 2 length | _____ |
| 3 height | _____ |
| 4 width | wide |

*2* The suffix *-en* is a common verb ending. It means *to make* or *to cause to become*. For example, the verb *sadden* means *to cause someone to become sad*. Sometimes you add this suffix to adjectives (*sad + en = sadden*). Other times you add this suffix to nouns (*strength + en = strengthen*).

Write down the verb form of the words on the left and the meaning of these verbs. Look at number 1 as an example.

| | VERB | MEANING |
|---|---|---|
| 1 deep | deepen | to make deeper |
| 2 length | _____ | _____ |
| 3 height | _____ | _____ |
| 4 wide | _____ | _____ |
| 5 short | _____ | _____ |

**Grammar focus**

| Jump! | **Don't worry** about it! |
|---|---|

*1* Below is some advice on learning to swim. Put a tick ( ✓ ) next to the advice if it is correct. Rewrite the advice if it is wrong.

1 Don't keep your legs straight when you kick. ☐ _____

2 Don't be afraid. ☐ _____

3 Keep your fingers together. ☐ _____

4 Open your mouth when your head is in the water. ☐ _____

5 Don't move your arms when you move your legs. ☐ _____

6 Go swimming straight after lunch. ☐ _____

**2** Write down three DOs and three DON'Ts for someone who is learning to
a) drive *or* b) play a game which you know

| DOs | DON'Ts |
| --- | --- |
| 1 | 4 |
| 2 | 5 |
| 3 | 6 |

**Writing task**

Describe a time when you had to do something of which you were very afraid.
Say:
- when it happened and where
- why you had to do it and how long it took you
- who was with you and how you felt with other(s) around
- how you felt when you finally did it and if you ever did it again

You may wish to include some of your conversation with the others who were
with you at the time.

# The Flying Fool

**What about you?**

1  What is the name of a hero/heroine from your country?
2  Why is this person famous?
3  How has your country honoured this person? Tick ( √) the appropriate box(es).

☐  a) a street named after him/her.

☐  b) a statue of him/her.

☐  c) a national holiday for his/her birthday.

☐  d) pictures of him/her in public buildings.

☐  e) souvenirs with his/her picture on it.

**Before you read**

The name of the man in the picture on the opposite page is Charles Lindbergh. He was a pilot. What do you know about him? What country was he from? Why is he famous?

Do this quiz on Charles Lindbergh. Put a circle around the correct answer. (If you do not know anything about Charles Lindbergh, try to guess the correct answer.)

1  Where did he fly?
   a) From St Louis to London
   b) From Boston to Rome
   c) From New York to Paris

2  When did he make his famous flight?
   a) 1919
   b) 1927
   c) 1939

3  What was the name of his plane?
   a) Concorde
   b) Apollo
   c) Spirit of St Louis

4  How long did the flight take?
   a) $9\frac{1}{4}$ hours
   b) $18\frac{3}{4}$ hours
   c) $33\frac{1}{2}$ hours

5  Which member of his family was kidnapped and murdered?
   a) His baby son
   b) His wife
   c) His mother

**Read the text**

Read the text. Did you answer all the questions in the quiz correctly?

# The Flying Fool

In 1919 a New York businessman offered a prize of $25,000 to whoever flew non-stop from New York to Paris for the first time. On 20 May 1927 Captain
5   Charles A. Lindbergh set out to win the prize. He took off from New York in a small, one-engined plane called 'Spirit of St Louis'. He took no map and no parachute. With him in the open cockpit
10   he had five sandwiches, two pints[1] of water and an inflatable raft. Some journalists reporting the story called him 'the flying fool'.

Thirty-three and a half hours later
15   Lindbergh landed safely at Le Bourget, near Paris. Americans went almost mad with joy. When Lindbergh returned to America a week later, half a million letters and 75,000 telegrams were
20   waiting for him. During a victory parade through New York, office workers gave him a 'ticker-tape welcome'. They threw confetti made of torn-up paper from their office windows. 1,800 tons[2] of paper
25   fell onto the streets along the route.

Lindbergh soon became America's greatest hero of the twentieth century. Hundreds of streets were renamed after him. He could not send his clothes to the
30   cleaners because laundry workers kept them for souvenirs. He could not write cheques because people kept them as autographs instead of cashing them. And the whole country mourned five
35   years later when his baby son was kidnapped and brutally murdered.

[1]*pint*: 0.57 of a litre
[2]*ton*: 1,000 kilogrammes

**Check your understanding**

**1** Match the definitions and pictures with words in the text. Write the words from the text in the blanks. Look at number 1 as an example.

1 a person who does something stupid  (*paragraph 1*)__*fool*__

2

(*paragraph 1*)__parachute__

3

(*paragraph 1*)_____

4 crazy  (*paragraph 2*)_____

5 an object a person keeps to remember a
place, an event, etc.  (*paragraph 3*)_____

6

(*paragraph 3*)_____

7 to feel and/or show sadness when
somebody dies  (*paragraph 3*)_____

**2** What do the following words refer to? Write your answers in the blanks. Look at number 1 as an example.

1 he (*line 6*)  __Lindbergh__    5 his (*line 29*)  _____

2 the prize (*line 6*) _____    6 them (*line 31*)  _____

3 him (*line 9*) _____    7 them (*line 32*)  _____

4 their (*line 24*) _____    8 the whole country (*line 34*) _____

**3** Put a cross (×) next to the subjects which the text does *not* mention.

1 _____ the prize for flying non-stop from New York to Paris

2 _____ why Lindbergh called his plane 'Spirit of St Louis'

3 _____ how Americans welcomed Lindbergh when he returned from Paris

4 _____ in which cities streets were named after Lindbergh

5 _____ what people who worked at cleaners did with Lindbergh's clothes

6 _____ the names of the people who kidnapped and killed Lindbergh's son

**What do you think?**

1 People often think that they would like to be famous. Do you think Lindbergh enjoyed being famous?

2 It was dangerous to fly across the Atlantic Ocean in the 1920s. Why do you think Lindbergh wanted to do it? Did he do it only for the money?

3 Can you think of any other people who have done something great but dangerous? What did they do? Would you like to do something like this?

**Vocabulary focus**

> Hundreds of streets were **renamed** after him.

The prefix *re-* often means *again*. *Rename* means *to name again*.
Do the crossword puzzle. The words with asterisks (*) begin with the prefix *re-*.
Look at '9 across' as an example.

## ACROSS

2* I don't like what I wrote. I'm going to _____ it.
7 1,000 kilogrammes
9* Her first husband died and she would like to _____ .
11 You are never _____ time.
12 Not cold
13 John is a _____'s name.
15* The bottle is empty again. Can you _____ it, please?
17 Margaret went _____ Scotland.
19 The plane took _____ at 9 pm.
21 Not there
22 What people say to a friend, for example, who has arrived for a visit to their country.

## DOWN

1 What you may get if you win a game or race.
2* The score was 0–0. They will _____ the match tomorrow.
3 I, you, he, she, _____ , they
4 Look! Do you see _____ ?
5 I'd like _____ fly a plane.
6 In Lindbergh's time aeroplanes had only one _____ .
8 Another word for happiness
9* Can you _____ the soup? It's cold.
10* People had to _____ their homes after the earthquake.
14* Next week we will _____ all the words which will be on the test.
16 Not high
18 It took Lindbergh _____ 33 hours to fly to Paris.
20 A number

*(crossword grid with 9 ACROSS answer filled in: r e m a r r y)*

## Grammar focus

k

| He touched down **safely**. | His son was **brutally** murdered. |

*Safely* (safe + ly) and *brutally* (brutal + ly) are both adverbs.

**1** Choose adverbs from the list on the right which you can use with the verbs on the left. Look at number 4 as an example.

1 drive _____ a) angrily
2 eat _____ b) badly
3 leave _____ c) carefully
4 listen  angrily, carefully, hard, happily, quietly _____ d) easily
5 rain _____ e) fast*
6 speak _____ f) happily
7 think _____ g) hard*
8 wait _____ h) quietly
9 walk _____ i) slowly
10 work _____ j) well*

* These adverb forms are irregular. The adjective forms are *fast, hard* and *good*.

**2** Check your answers. Then write down other adverbs which you could use with the verbs in Exercise 1.

_____  _____  _____  _____

_____  _____  _____  _____

## Writing task

Write a description of a famous person from your country. Say:
• when he or she lived
• why he or she is famous
• what this person did in his or her lifetime
Give as many details as possible.

# Phone Card

**What about you?**

1 What do you need to make a call from a payphone in your country, e.g. a special coin/a credit card?

2 Where can you find payphones in your country? Are they in phoneboxes?

3 Is the payphone system in your country good? Do the phones always work?

**Before you read**

1 Look at the picture below. What do you think a 'Phonecard' is? _____

_____

2 This advertisement has three sections. These sections are called:

   a) What do you do with it?

   b) Now appearing in a shop near you.

   c) No more broken payphones.

Which section do you think will be about:

Why Phonecards are good? _____

How you use a Phonecard? _____

Where you can get a Phonecard? _____

**Read the text**

Read the advertisement quickly. (Time limit: one minute)

   a) Did you guess what a 'Phonecard' was?

   b) Did you guess what the three sections were about?

How many coins have you got in your pocket right now?
   Three? Two? A bent **one**?
   With a Phonecard you can make up to 200 calls without any change at all.

*What do you do with **it**?*

5    Go to a telephone box marked (you guessed it) 'Phonecard.' Slot[1] in your card, make your call and when you've finished, a screen tells you how much is left on your card.

    It costs no extra for the cards, and the calls cost 10p per unit, the same as any other payphone call.

10    You can buy **them** in units of 10, 20, 40, 100 or 200.

[1]*slot*: put

*Now appearing in a shop near you*
Near each Cardphone location[2] you'll find a shop where you can buy **one**.
**They**'re at bus, train and inner city tube stations.
Many universities, hospitals and clubs. Motorway service areas[3] and shopping
15  centres.
At airports and seaports.

*No more broken payphones*
Most broken payphones are like **that** because **they**'ve been vandalised[4].
There are no coins in a Cardphone to attract thieves. So you're less likely to
20  find a vandalised **one**.
Get a Phonecard yourself and try **it** out. Or get a bigger wallet.

[2]*location*: place
[3]*motorway service areas*: places on motorways that have restaurants and petrol stations
[4]*vandalised*: damaged or destroyed

**Check your understanding**

**1** Look at the words in **bold** print in the advertisement. Draw an arrow (→) to the words to which they refer.

*Example:* How many coins have you got in your pocket right now?
Three? Two? A bent **one**?

**2** In this exercise there is another advertisement for a Phonecard, but it is not complete or correct. Read the text on pages 38–9 again.

1 Put the pictures under 'How you use it' in the correct order. Write the correct number in each box under the picture.
2 Fill in each blank under 'How much it costs' and 'Why you should have a Phonecard' with the correct information.

## How you use it

Put in your phonecard

Look at the screen to find out how many calls you can still make

Go to a telephone box marked 'Phonecard'

Make your call

## How much it costs:

One unit = _____ p
A card with
  20 units = £ _____
  40 units = £ _____
  100 units = £ _____
  200 units = £ _____

## Why you should have a phonecard:

You don't need any _____ .
There will be fewer _____ payphones.

*3* Advertisements expect you to understand certain things although they don't say them clearly. Read the statement in *italics* from the Phonecard advertisement. Then fill in the blanks with one of the statements below. (Be careful! There is one extra answer.)

a) Phonecards are cheap.
b) You cannot use all payphones.
c) People do not like carrying a lot of coins.
d) Phonecards are easy to find.
e) Thieves will not break Cardphones.

1 *Go to a telephone box marked 'Phonecard'.* This statement means

_____

2 *Now appearing in a shop near you.* This statement means

_____

3 *You're less likely to find a broken one.* This statement means

_____

4 *Or get a bigger wallet.* This statement means

_____

**What do you think?**

1 After reading this advertisement, would you buy a Phonecard? Why?/Why not?
2 Can you think of any problems there might be if you can only use a payphone with a Phonecard?
3 What do you think are the three most important inventions of the twentieth century. What are their good and bad points?

**Vocabulary focus**

> Go to a telephone box marked . . . 'Phonecard'.
> No more broken **payphones**.

*Payphone* is a compound word made up of the words *pay* and *phone*.
*Phonebox* is a compound word made up of the words *phone* and *box*.

*1* Make as many compound words as you can from the following list.

clip    paper    nail    phones    finger    phone    dryer
hair    coat    rain    cloth    face    card    head

*2* Use some of the words you have made to complete the following sentences.

1 Where's my _____ ? It looks like it's going to rain.
2 I always use my _____ to make phone calls; it's more convenient than coins.
3 Where's the _____ ? I'm going to wash my hair.
4 We don't want to hear the football match. Why don't you use your _____ to listen to it?
5 A _____ is less likely to be vandalised than a coin box.

## Grammar focus

> Go to a phonebox that works, not a broken **one**.
> Do you have any 10p coins? I only have bent **ones**.

*1* Fill in the dialogues with correct answers. Look at the example.

*Example:*
A: I'm looking for a red jumper in size 14.
B: We have two in your size.
A: I'd like ___the long-sleeved one.___
   *or*
A: I'd like ___the one with long sleeves.___

long sleeved/
with long sleeves
✓

short sleeved/
with short sleeves
✗

1  A: I'm looking for some blue coffee mugs.
   B: We have two kinds.
   A: I'd like _____
      *or*
   A: I'd like _____

striped/
with stripes
✓

spotted/
with spots
✗

2  A: I'm looking for a green T-shirt.
   B: We have two styles.
   A: I'd like _____
      *or*
   A: I'd like _____

v-necked/
with a v-neck
✗

round-necked
with a round neck
✓

3  A: I'd like some black socks.
   B: We have two kinds.
   A: I'd like _____

long
✗

short
✓

*2* Fill in the blanks using your own ideas and *one* or *ones*.

1 If you like the black trousers so much, why are you going to buy _____ ?
2 Put the potatoes in the big dish not _____ .
3 Which shoes do you like better, _____ or _____ ?
4 Are you going to see the film with Paul Newman? No, _____ .

## Writing task

Write a description of a Phonecard. Say:
 • what it is
 • how it works
 • how much it costs
 • why people should use it

# Splitting the Image

**What about you?**

Look at the picture of the identical twins. Put a tick ( ✓ ) next to the statements with which you agree.

1 Their first names begin with the same letter. ☐

2 Their mother dresses them in identical clothes. ☐

3 They do everything together. ☐

4 Each one knows what the other one is thinking. ☐

5 They have the same habits. ☐

*Mike and Martin Henfield.*

**Before you read**

*Mike and Martin Henfield*

Look at the picture of the same identical twins as adults. In the text you are going to read, Martin Henfield, the man on the right, talks about some of his experiences as an identical twin. Write down five words you expect to read in the text.

1 _____

2 _____

3 _____

4 _____

5 _____

**Read the text**

Read the text. Does it contain the words which you wrote down?

# SPLITTING THE IMAGE

When we were small my mother used to dress us in identical clothes. That was bad enough. But when we went on our first camping trip with the scouts[1] she went one better. We were only ten or so, and while all the other boys settled down for the night in their sleeping
5   bags, we were very embarrassed when we had to snuggle inside a special double sleeping bag my mother had made for us out of two blankets.

At school we were known as Henfield One and Henfield Two. We both had the same middle name, Owen, so people couln't even
10   distinguish us by our initials as both of us were M.O. It was only when I went to college and began to have my own separate set of friends that I started to feel my own freedom of identity.

[1]*the scouts* (the Boy Scouts): the name of an organisation for boys

Before I went to college, during the sixth-form[2] holidays, I got a job on a building site. Mike didn't work. He was resting. One week I said
15 to the foreman, 'Can I have a week off?' 'Certainly,' he said, 'but you won't have a job when you get back.' It was really hard work, mainly carrying sand and bricks. On the Friday night, I said to my brother, 'Would you like to earn a week's money?' And he said, yes. So I told him about everything. Where the sand was, where the bricks were;
20 and I described the eight workmen. On Monday morning, he went down in my jeans, jacket and woolly hat. He worked there all week and none of them knew the difference. Two years later I met the foreman in a pub and I bought him a drink. I told him the story, but he just laughed and said he didn't believe me. There was no way I could
25 convince him.
Now I feel very different from my brother. We still come together for some things but I feel quite remote from him. And he'll tell you the same. I suppose we have really been working towards that for forty-two years.

[2]*sixth-form*: the last year of secondary school

**Check your understanding**

**1** Imagine that each paragraph of the text had a title. Choose a title for each paragraph from the list below. Write the number of the paragraph in each box. (Be careful! There is one extra title.)

a) ☐  Our parents

b) ☐  The good times

c) ☐  The bad times

d) ☐  A separate life

e) ☐  Who am I?

**2** Fill in each blank with one of the words listed below. (Be careful! There are three extra choices.)

a) embarrassed (*line 5*)    d) distinguish (*line 10*)    g) foreman (*line 15*)
b) snuggle (*line 5*)    e) initials (*line 10*)    h) convince (*line 25*)
c) blankets (*line 7*)    f) identity (*line 12*)    i) remote (*line 27*)

1 You don't have to write your first name and surname. Just write your

_____ .

2 You can _____ the twins by their voices. Ann's is much lower than Alice's.

3 It is difficult to _____ children that sweets are not good for them.

4 The man has an _____ problem. He doesn't know who he really is.

5 Put some more _____ on the bed. It's cold tonight.

6 I was very _____ when I arrived at the meeting an hour late.

**3** Read the third paragraph again. Then put the sentences below in the correct order by writing numbers 1 to 12 in the boxes.

☐ a) Martin asked Mike if he wanted to work for a week.

☐ b) The foreman said that that couldn't be true and laughed.

☐ c) Martin met the foreman in a pub and they started talking.

☐ d) Martin got a summer job.

☐ e) The foreman and all the workers thought that Mike was Martin.

☐ f) Martin was tired and asked the foreman for a week's holiday.

☐ g) Mike worked for a week and Martin had a rest.

☐ h) Mike said yes.

☐ i) The foreman said no.

☐ j) Martin told the foreman that his identical twin brother had worked in his place when the foreman said he couldn't have a week off.

☐ k) Martin told Mike all about the job and the people.

☐ l) When Martin returned to work after his rest, nobody knew he hadn't been there the week before.

**What do you think?**

1  What are the advantages and disadvantages of being a twin?
2  Do you know any (identical) twins? Can you distinguish one from the other? Do they have similar habits? (Or, if you have a twin brother or sister, can people distinguish the two of you? Do you have similar habits?)
3  Describe a time in the past when it would have been nice to have had an identical twin to go somewhere you didn't want to go?

**Vocabulary focus**

| I **got** a job |

K

**1** The word *get* has many meanings. Decide on the correct meaning of *get* as it is used in each of the sentences in Column A. Write the correct letter from Column B in each box. Look at number 1 as an example.

COLUMN **A**

1  We *got into* our sleeping bags.

2  I will be asleep when you *get back*.

3  We still *get together* for some things.

4  I *got* a letter from my brother yesterday.

5  When twins *get* older, they usually go their separate ways.

6  We *got* there late.

COLUMN **B**

[C] a)  arrive

☐ b)  become

☐ c)  enter

☐ d)  receive

☐ e)  have a meeting or party

☐ f)  return

*2* Answer the questions truthfully.

1 What time did you get to school (or work) today? _____

2 Have you got anything in the post recently? _____

3 Do you usually fall asleep immediately after you get into bed? _____

4 How often do you get together with friends? _____

5 Does it get cold or warm at this time of year in your country? _____

6 What time did you get back home last night? _____

## Grammar focus

| My mother **used to dress** us in identical clothes. |
| --- |

We use *used to + verb* to talk about:
- frequent events in the past which do not happen any more: *My mother used to dress us in identical clothes.*
- situations which are no longer true: *We used to have the same friends.*

The negative form is *didn't use to + verb*. The question form is *Did (you) use to + verb.*

*1* Put a tick ( ✓) next to the statements which were true for you.

When I was a young child:

1 I used to drink a lot of milk. ☐

2 I used to watch children's programmes on TV. ☐

3 I didn't use to go to the shops alone. ☐

4 I used to like listening to people tell me stories. ☐

5 I didn't use to stay up late at night. ☐

6 I used to sleep for a few hours in the afternoon. ☐

*2* Write down true sentences about your childhood with *used to/didn't use to + verb.*
(What you used to eat and what you didn't use to eat)

1 _____

2 _____

(What you used to do in the summer and what you didn't use to do)

3 _____

4 _____

## Writing task

Write about a funny or embarrassing experience from your childhood. Say:
- when it happened and whom you were with
- exactly what happened
- how you felt at the time
- how you feel about it now

# Warning! Don't Go near the Water

**What about you?**

1 If you can swim, how often do you go swimming? Where do you usually swim – in the sea, in a pool, in a river, in a lake or somewhere else?
2 Swimming can be dangerous. What are the two most important things people should remember when they go swimming?

**Before you read**

What is the title of the article? What do you think the article is about? Are the following statements true or false? Put a circle around the correct answer.

1 Being able to swim will protect you from drowning.   TRUE/FALSE
2 The sea is the most dangerous water of all to swim in.   TRUE/FALSE
3 Women are more likely to[1] drown than men.   TRUE/FALSE
4 Freak waves[2] often cause deaths off beaches.   TRUE/FALSE
5 You can 'waterproof' babies[3] by teaching them to swim early.   TRUE/FALSE

> [1]*likely to*: probably
> [2]*freak waves*: sudden high waves
> [3]*'waterproof' babies*: make sure that babies do not drown

**Read the text**

Read the article. Did you circle the correct answers?

> # WARNING!
>
> ## Don't go near the water!
>
> 1 Swimming ability may not protect you against drowning; well over half the people who drown in Britain each year can swim.
> 5 Swimming in warm indoor pools is different from cold outdoor water.
> 2 The figures show that the sea is not the most common scene of drownings. Rivers and streams
> 10 account for more deaths. And the total number drowned in inland[1] waters is double those off the coast[2]. More people are rescued off beaches, where their difficulties
> 15 tend to be noticed. Lakes and rivers are more isolated.
> 3 More than three times as many men as women drown each year. Of the 535 drowned in the UK last
> 20 year, 411 were men. Highest figures are for males between
> fifteen and twenty-five – who tend to take most risks.
> 4 'When you are at the seaside,
> 25 the thing to remember about so-called freak waves is that they are just not that freaky[3],' says Tom Sanders, water safety adviser of the Royal Society for the Prevention
> 30 of Accidents. 'Such waves are described so often to explain mishaps off British coasts that we should expect sudden high waves every few minutes.'
> 35 5 It's dangerous nonsense to think you can 'waterproof' a baby against drowning, say RSPA – it's about as realistic as saying that once toddlers can walk twenty
> 40 yards[4] they are safe to cross the road.

> [1]*inland*: inside the country, not near the sea
> [2]*coast*: the land next to the sea
> [3]*freaky*: unusual
> [4]*yard*: a little less than a metre

**1** Match the words in Column A with the correct meaning in Column B. Write the correct letter from Column B in each box. (Be careful! There are two extra choices in Column B.)

COLUMN **A**                          COLUMN **B**

1 common (*line 8*)  ☐        a) a child who has just learnt to walk

2 rescued (*line 13*) ☐        b) an accident

3 noticed (*line 15*) ☐        c) swam

4 isolated (*line 16*) ☐        d) usual

5 males (*line 21*)  ☐        e) when

6 mishap (*line 32*) ☐        f) saved

7 once (*line 39*)  ☐        g) seen

8 toddler (*line 39*) ☐        h) men and boys

                                      i) women and girls

                                      j) without many people around

**2** The graph and chart below accompanied the article. However, some information is missing from them. Fill in each blank with the correct word or number. (You will need to use maths to answer questions 2, 3 and 4.)

1 Write *coastal areas* and *home baths* in the correct blanks in the pie chart.
2 Write down the percentage (%) of people who drown in coastal areas and the percentage of people who drown in their bath at home. (Note that lakes, reservoirs, canals, docks, ponds, rivers and streams are all 'inland waters'.)
3 Fill in the second line of the table with the total number of drownings for people between the ages of 15 and 24.
4 Fill in the fourth line of the table with the number of drownings of males (m) and females (f) in the 15–24 age group.

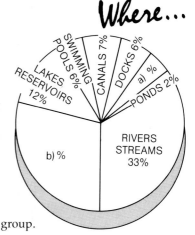

*Where...*

SWIMMING POOLS 6%
CANALS 7%
DOCKS 6%
LAKES RESERVOIRS 12%
a) %
PONDS 2%
RIVERS STREAMS 33%
b) %

*Who...*

| AGE | UNDER 5 | 5–14 | 15–24 | 25–34 | 35–44 | 45–54 | 55–64 | 65+ |
|---|---|---|---|---|---|---|---|---|
| **DROWNINGS** | 40 | 37 | c) | 71 | 74 | 60 | 51 | 82 |
| **SEX** | m f 30 10 | m f 29 8 | m f d) e) | m f 65 6 | m f 55 19 | m f 50 10 | m f 36 15 | m f 45 37 |

**3** Below is some good swimming advice. However, not all of it is connected to the information in the article. Put a ( √ ) tick next to that advice which *is* connected to the information in the article.

1  Be careful even if you are a good swimmer. ☐

2  Never swim immediately after you have eaten. ☐

3  If you want to be really safe, swim in a pool and not in the sea. ☐

4  If you swim in a river or lake, make sure you are with other people. ☐

5  Learn how to save people who are in trouble in the water. ☐

6  Be careful in the sea, where there are often dangerous high waves. ☐

7  Watch all young children in the water at all times. ☐

8  Learn to swim when you are young. ☐

**What do you think?**

1  Did anything in this article surprise you?
2  Do you think all the information in the article would interest people from your country? If not, what information do you think they would find interesting?
3  Can you think of any other information you think this article should mention?

**Vocabulary focus**

> Being **able** to swim will protect you.
> Swimming **ability** may not protect you.

**1** Fill in the blanks in the box with the verb, noun, adjective or adverb form of the words in the box. If you do not know the forms, use a dictionary. Look at number 1 as an example.

| | VERB | NOUN | ADJECTIVE | ADVERB |
|---|---|---|---|---|
| 1 | | _ability_ | able | |
| 2 | | accident | _____ | _____ |
| 3 | endanger | _____ | dangerous | _____ |
| 4 | _____ | death | | |
| 5 | | difficulty | _____ | |
| 6 | explain | _____ | | |
| 7 | _____ | prevention | | |
| 8 | protect | _____ | | |
| 9 | | _____ | realistic | _____ |
| 10 | _____ | safety | _____ | _____ |
| 11 | _____ | _____ | warm | _____ |

**2** Fill in each blank with one of the words from the box above.

1  There are more _____ from car accidents than there are from drowning.

2  I hit him _____ . I didn't know he was there.

3  We _____ our hands over the fire when we came in from the cold.

4  Without her glasses, she sees with _____ .

5  People could _____ accidents if they drove more slowly.

48

> Lakes and rivers are **more isolated than** beaches.
> The sea is **the most dangerous** water of all.

**1** Write the comparative (*more isolated, bigger*) and superlative (*the most isolated, the biggest*) forms of the adjectives in the correct columns below. Look at the examples.

| bad | common | easy | high | safe |
|-----|--------|------|------|------|
| big | dangerous | good | isolated | warm |
| cold | different | healthy | pretty | young |

| -ER THAN | -IER THAN | MORE . . . THAN | IRREGULAR |
|----------|-----------|-----------------|-----------|
| bigger than | | more isolated than | |
| THE -EST | THE -IEST | THE MOST . . . | IRREGULAR |
| the biggest | | the most isolated | |

**2** Fill in each blank with the correct form of one of the adjectives below. Add *than* or *the* where necessary. Look at numbers 1 and 2 as examples.

| bad | difficult | good | safe |
|-----|-----------|------|------|
| dangerous | easy | healthy | warm |

1 Water in a pool is usually ___**warmer than**___ water in the sea.
2 Swimming in an isolated river is one of ___**the most dangerous**___ places to swim.
3 Swimming in a pool is _____ swimming in a lake or river.
4 _____ time to go swimming is immediately after you have eaten.
5 All exercise is good for you, but swimming is _____ exercise of all.
6 Taking exercise at least once a week is _____ taking no exercise at all.
7 The article in this unit was _____ the reading in Unit Nine.

**Writing task**

Make a sign for a swimming area near your city or in your city. In this sign:
- say what people must not do in the area (for example, 'Do not play ball')
- give people as much advice as possible about what they should do and should not do in the water (for example, 'Do not swim alone')

**What about you?**

1 When you see an advertisement in a newspaper or magazine, do you read it? Why?/Why not?
2 When there are advertisements on TV, do you watch them? Why?/Why not?
3 What is the best advertisement you have ever seen or read?

**Before you read**

In this unit you are going to read an advertisement. Look at the pictures from the advertisement at the bottom of the page. What do you think the advertisement is for? Tick ( ✓ ) the appropriate box.

1 ☐ a cassette recorder company     4 ☐ a bank

2 ☐ a new record and cassette     5 ☐ other (What? _____ )

3 ☐ a hat company

**Read the text**

Read the text. Did you guess what the advertisement was for?

There was a young chap from Stoke.
Who found he was always broke.
Then an 'On Line' account.
Helped him save an amount.
5 And now he's a different bloke.

You'll be able to manage your money more effectively[1] with a NatWest On Line account. All you need to open one is a fiver.

Three pounds of that starts you saving. The rest brings
10 you special On Line exclusives[2] like our regular news magazine, packed with pop, fashion, sport and competitions.

You also receive a slimline electronic 'continuous memory' calculator in its own stylish wallet[3].
15 Just the thing for counting up the cash you'll save with On Line.

**Account opening requirements and conditions must be complied with. Terms and conditions may vary. Seven days notice of withdrawal required to avoid loss of interest.**
20      **Registered office – 41 Lothbury, London EC2P 2BP.**

[1] *more effectively*: better
[2] *exclusives*: special gifts
[3] *wallet*: a small flat leather or plastic container

**1** Put a circle around the correct answer.

1 *Chap* (informal) (*line 1*) and
  *bloke* (informal) (*line 5*) mean
  a) a baby
  b) a man
2 *Broke* (*line 2*) means
  a) without money
  b) without friends
3 *Account* (*line 3*) means
  a) money kept in a bank
  b) person who works in a bank

4 *Save* (*line 4*) means
  a) give money to friends
  b) keep money
5 *Manage* (*line 6*) means
  a) find
  b) control

**2** Complete the information in the box with words from the poem. Look at number 1 as an example.

| | |
|---|---|
| 1 What city was the man from? | Stoke |
| 2 What was the man's problem? | _____ |
| 3 What did he get? | _____ |
| 4 How has he changed? | _____ |

**3** Gill has gone to the National Westminster Bank to ask about an On Line account. Below is part of her conversation with the bank manager. Fill in the manager's answers with the correct information from the advertisement.

Gill: How much do I need to open an account, £5 or £3?

Manager: _____

Gill: How much of that goes into my account?

Manager: _____

Gill: And is it true that with the rest of the money I get a magazine, a calculator and a wallet for the calculator?

Manager: _____

**4** There are three sections in the 'On Line' advertisement, and each of these sections has a different purpose. Match the purposes on the left with the correct section of the advertisement on the right. Write the correct letter of the section in each box. (Be careful! There is one extra purpose.)

*PURPOSE*

1 to tell you about possible problems

2 to make you interested in the subject of the advertisement

3 to give you information about National Westminster Bank

4 to give you specific information about the good points of an On Line account

*SECTION*

☐ a) *lines 1–5*

☐ b) *lines 6–16*

☐ c) *lines 17–20*

☐

**What do you think?**

1  Would you open an On Line account? Why?/Why not?
2  Which section of the advertisement has informal language? Which has the most formal language? Why do you think there is this difference?
3  Is the advertisement for young people or families? How do you know?
4  How do banks advertise in your country?

**Vocabulary focus**

Just the thing for counting up the **cash** you'll save

*1* How many of the *money* words below do you know? Read the definitions. Then fill in each blank with one of the words.

cash      change      cheque      coin      credit card      note

1 _____ Money which is made of paper.

2 _____ Money which is made of metal.

3 _____ What you get if a shirt costs £17.99 and you give the shop assistant £20.

4 _____ A printed piece of paper which you write on. You can buy things with this. You can also get money for it at a bank.

5 _____ A plastic card you can use to buy things. You pay the money for what you bought after one or two months.

6 _____ Coins and paper money.

*2* Answer the questions.

1  Do you have any cash in your pocket or wallet? _____

2  Do you have a cheque or credit card with you? _____

3  What are the names of the credit cards in your country? _____

4  How do people usually pay for things in your country – by cash, cheque or credit card? _____

5  In the UK there are, for example, one-pound coins and five-pound notes. What are the notes and coins in your country? _____

**Grammar focus**

You'll be able to manage your **money** more effectively.

There are some words which we count (*one book, two books*) and some words which we do not count (*money*). Words we do not count in English do **not** have a plural form and do **not** take a plural verb.

*1* Look at the words in the list below. If we count the word in English, put a C. If we do not count the word, put a *U*.

| | | | |
|---|---|---|---|
| 1 ☐ feet | 5 ☐ hair | 9 ☐ money | 13 ☐ teeth |
| 2 ☐ food | 6 ☐ information | 10 ☐ music | 14 ☐ weather |
| 3 ☐ fruit | 7 ☐ knowledge | 11 ☐ people | |
| 4 ☐ furniture | 8 ☐ medicine | 12 ☐ sunshine | |

*2* Look at the words which have *U* in Exercise 1. Which of these words have a plural form in your language? Write these words in the blanks.

_____  _____  _____  _____  _____

_____  _____  _____  _____  _____

*3* Fill in the blanks with *is, isn't, are* or *aren't.*

1 Where _____ the money?

2 Your feet _____ dirty and your hair _____ too. You need a bath.

3 This information _____ very useful. Go back and ask them again.

4 The food _____ on the table. Let's eat.

5 All of the furniture in her house _____ brown.

6 Fruit _____ good for you.

7 This medicine _____ good for stomach pains.

8 Some people _____ waiting for you in the office. Will you be long?

**Writing task**

Imagine that you want to open an On Line account by post. Write a letter to National Westminster Bank. In your letter say:
- that you have seen an advertisement for an On Line account
- that you would like to open an account
- how much you are enclosing
- that you are looking forward to receiving the magazine and calculator

Begin your letter like this:

your address<br>your city<br>today's date

National Westminster Bank,
8 Plane Road,
Finchley,
London N10.

Dear Sir or Madam,
    I have recently seen an advertisement for an On Line account and . . .

# Half a Croissant and a Hot Water Bottle

**What about you?**

1 What kind of music do you like? (Pop? Rock? Jazz? Classical? Traditional music from your country?)
2 Who is your favourite singer or group?

**Before you read**

The name of the singer on the opposite page is Sade. You are going to read an interview with her. Read the questions which the interviewer asked her.

1 What do you miss most about England when you're away? _____

2 What do you always take with you on tour[1]? _____

3 Do you send many postcards? _____

4 Do you call your mum much[2]? _____

5 What do you have for breakfast when you're away? _____

6 Do you protect[3] your voice when you're on tour? _____

7 Do you do a lot of interviews abroad? _____

> [1]*on tour*: a singer's trips to different countries
> [2]*call your mum much*: telephone your mother often
> [3]*protect*: to keep safe; to keep in good condition

What do you think her answers were? Write them in the blanks or discuss them with another student.

**Read the text**

1 The questions (above) are missing from the interview on the opposite page. Read the text and write the questions in the correct blanks. (The questions are not in the correct order.)
2 Did you predict what Sade said?

**Check your understanding**

**1** Put a circle around the correct answer.

1 *It* (*line 7*) means
   a) the hot water bottle
   b) the air conditioning

2 *They* (*line 14*) means
   a) hot water bottles
   b) vitamins

3 *It* (*line 20*) means
   a) breakfast
   b) an orange

4 *It* (*line 45*) means
   a) sitting
   b) talking about yourself for two hours

5 *The place* (*line 60*) means
   a) England
   b) Spain

6 *That* (*line 70*) means
   a) singing in front of strangers in a foreign country
   b) singing in front of your aunties when you're fourteen

# Half a Croissant & a Hot Water Bottle

1) _____?
Potters' Catarrh Pastels[1] and a hot water bottle.

The water bottle is very important because all these hotels have air conditioning and it messes my throat up completely. So I don't have the heat on. I just have my hot water bottle.

Another essential on tour is my vitamins. I never take them but it's reassuring to know that they're there.

2) _____?
I started our world tour with great intentions – poached egg on toast, muesli[2], tea and an orange every day – but now it's waning[3]. I'll get through half a croissant and go for the extra lie-in.

3) _____?
Yes, I do. And she calls me – usually just before we're about to go on stage. I make an effort to call because when you're away you create a whole life around you. You're not nearly as aware of how long you've been away as somebody who is doing the same thing every day.

4) _____?
No. When the group first started I told my mother I'd send her a postcard from wherever we visited. I sent her ones from Hawaii, Ireland and Belgium this time – then I gave up!

5) _____?
I try to do as few as possible. If you sit for two hours a day talking about yourself it's pretty unnatural. Most people probably only talk for that long in the whole day – with a few exceptions!

6) _____?
Yes, basically I just keep my throat covered. Also I don't have ice in drinks or hot soup. That's a real problem in America where even the towels come in ice!

7) _____?
I miss England. The atmosphere. Just everything about the place. I can't imagine living anywhere else but I would like to buy a place in Spain.

It's much more frightening singing at home because you're so close to everyone. I'm glad I was never one of those girls who had to sing in front of her aunties when she was fourteen. That must be terrifying.

---

[1]*Potters' Catarrh Pastels*: a kind of medicine for the throat
[2]*muesli*: a kind of breakfast cereal
[3]*it's waning*: it's getting less and less

**2** Match the words in Column A with their meanings in Column B. Write the correct letter from Column B in each box. (Be careful. There is one extra answer.)

COLUMN **A**

1 mess up (*line 7*)

2 essential (*line 11*)

3 intention (*line 17*)

4 lie-in (*line 22*)

5 (be) aware (*line 30*)

6 give up (*line 41*)

7 unnatural (*line 46*)

8 frightening (*line 64*)

COLUMN **B**

☐ a) a plan

☐ b) making someone feel afraid

☐ c) extra time in bed in the morning

☐ d) something necessary

☐ e) money

☐ f) to cause something to be in bad condition

☐ g) to stop

☐ h) to know

☐ i) different from what usually happens

**3** Below is a newspaper article about Sade. There are four facts in it which are wrong. <u>Underline</u> the facts which are wrong.

# The World of Sade

In a recent interview with Sade she talked about her health and how she takes care of herself when she is on tour. She always takes medicine for her throat, vitamins and her own hot water bottle with her. She does not use the heating system in hotels because it is bad for her throat. She also said that she makes sure she eats lots of hot food like soup but never has drinks that are very cold. Sade talked about the importance of a good breakfast and knew that she should eat more than half a croissant. However, she likes to sleep late in the morning and does not have enough time to eat more.

Sade is very close to her family. She speaks to her mother often when she is on tour and sends her postcards from every place she visits. She loves England very much, but she loves Spain even more and hopes to buy a place there. Finally, Sade explained that she does not like to do many interviews because talking a lot is bad for her throat.

## What do you think?

1 What sort of person is Sade?
2 Is she like other pop stars? Is she like you expect a pop star to be?
3 Is there anything you like about her? Is there anything you don't like?
4 Imagine you are going to interview your favourite singer or film star. Write down four questions you would like to ask.

## Vocabulary focus

> I would like to buy a **place** in Spain.

**1** Look at the pictures below. Which place do you think Sade would like to buy?

1 _____

2 _____

3 _____

4 _____

5 _____

6 _____

7 _____

*K*

**2** Below is a list of different types of places. Write the correct word under each picture on page 56.

| | | | |
|---|---|---|---|
| castle | flat | mansion | villa |
| block of flats | house | palace | |

*K*

**3** Write down how each of these places is different from the other. Look at number 5 as an example.

1 a castle: _____

2 a block of flats: _____

3 a flat: _____

4 a house: _____

5 a mansion: <u>very large, usually for rich people.</u> _____

6 a palace: _____

7 a villa: _____

**Grammar focus**

*K*

> Just **everything** about the place.
> I can't imagine living **anywhere** else.
> You're so close to **everyone**.

**1** Choose the correct word from the list below and fill in the blanks. (In some sentences there are two correct answers.)

| | | | |
|---|---|---|---|
| somebody | someone | something | somewhere |
| nobody | no one | nothing | nowhere |
| anybody | anyone | anything | anywhere |
| everybody | everyone | everything | everywhere |

1 It is difficult to talk to people who think they know _____ .

2 _____ is in the other room, but I don't know her name.

3 I can't talk to _____ for a few hours. I have a lot of work to do.

4 There is _____ good on TV tonight. Let's go to the cinema.

5 _____ came to the party except George. I was glad they could all come.

6 We haven't got _____ for dinner. Why don't we go out for a meal?

7 Can I talk to you for a minute? I'd like to ask you _____ .

8 We're not going _____ on holiday this summer. Everything's too expensive.

**Writing task**

If you like Sade's music, write her a letter. If you have never heard Sade's music before, write a letter to one of your favourite singers.

- Say why you like his/her music.
- Ask anything you would like to know about his/her life.

Begin your letter like this:

your address,
your city,
today's date

Dear (Sade),

I love all your music and am writing to you because I wanted you to know this. I also. . .

# UNIT **13** Little House on the Prairie

**What about you?**

Look at the picture from this unit's reading and answer the questions.

1 In what country do you think the story takes place?
2 When do you think the story takes place?
3 What exactly is happening in the picture? What do you think this part of the story is about?

**Before you read**

[1]*howl*: to make a long loud cry, especially that made by dogs
[2]*jerk*: to pull suddenly
[3]*rope*:

Read these sentences from the text. Then fill in the blanks with the names of the parents, the children and the animals.

1 Baby Carrie was playing on the floor in the sunshine.
2 'Get the tub full of water!' Pa shouted. 'Put sacks in it! Hurry!'
3 Ma told Laura to stay at the house.
4 Mary and Laura stood against the house and held hands.
5 Jack howled[1].
6 Bunny and Pet and Patty were jerking[2] at the ropes[3].

| PARENTS | CHILDREN | ANIMALS |
|---------|----------|---------|
| —— | —— | —— —— |
| —— | —— | —— —— |

**Read the text**

Read the first section of the text. Then stop and answer the question. After you have written down your answer, read the next section. If your answer was correct, put a tick ( √ ) next to it. Do the same with the other sections.

[1]*it is going to storm*: there is going to be a lot of rain and wind
[2]*billowing up*: rising up

> Baby Carrie was playing on the floor in the sunshine, and suddenly the sunshine was gone.
>   'I do believe it is going to storm[1],' Ma
> 5 said, looking out of the window. Laura looked, too, and great clouds were billowing up[2] in the south, across the sun.

1 What do you think is going to happen next? ☐ ——————
Now read on and see if you were right.

³*plough*:

⁴*prairie*: a wide, flat piece of land with grass but without trees

Pet and Patty were coming running from the field, Pa holding to the heavy plough³

10    and bounding in long leaps behind it.

'Prairie⁴ fire!' he shouted. 'Get the tub full of water! Put sacks in it! Hurry!'

**2 What is Pa going to do?** ☐ _____

Now read on and see if you were right.

Pa was ploughing, shouting at Pet and Patty to make them hurry. The sky was

15    black now, the air was as dark as if the sun had set. Pa ploughed a long furrow⁵ west of the house, and back again east of the house. He tied Pet and Patty to the other north corner of the house.

20        The wind was rising and wildly screaming. Thousands of birds flew before the fire, thousands of rabbits were running.

Pa was going along the furrow, setting fire to the grass on the other side of it. Ma

25    followed with a wet sack, beating at the flames that tried to cross the furrow. The whole prairie was hopping with rabbits. Snakes rippled across the yard. Prairie hens ran silently. Birds screamed in the

30    screaming wind.

**3 What did the children do?** ☐ _____

Now read on.

⁵*furrow*:

The prairie fire was roaring now, roaring louder and louder. Mary and Laura stood against the house and held hands and trembled⁶. Baby Carrie was in the house.

35    Laura wanted to do something, but inside her head was a roaring and whirling like the fire. Her middle shook, and tears poured out of her stinging⁷ eyes. Her eyes and her nose and her throat stung with smoke.

40        Jack howled. Bunny and Pet and Patty were jerking at the ropes and squealing horribly. The orange, yellow, terrible flames were coming faster than horses can run, and their quivering light danced over

45    everything.

The wind rose to a high, crackling, rushing shriek, flames climbed into the crackling air. Fire was all around the house.

⁶*tremble*: to shake

⁷*sting*: to burn

**Check your understanding**

*k*

**1** Put a circle around the best title for the text.

1 My Pa     2 Animals Everywhere     3 Prairie Fire

**2** Some of the words below describe a type of sound. The other words describe a type of movement. Write Sound (S) or Movement (M) in the boxes. (If you do not know the meaning of the word, try to guess its meaning from the story. Or, say the word to yourself and guess from the sound of the word.)

1 shout (*line 11*) ☐          6 hop (*line 27*) ☐          11 squeal (*line 41*) ☐

2 rise (*lines 20 and 46*) ☐     7 ripple (*line 28*) ☐     12 quiver (*line 44*) ☐

3 scream (*lines 21 and 30*) ☐   8 roar (*line 31*) ☐        13 crackle (*line 46*) ☐

4 fly (*line 21*) ☐              9 whirl (*line 36*) ☐        14 rush (*line 47*) ☐

5 run (*lines 22 and 29*) ☐      10 jerk (*line 41*) ☐        15 climb (*line 47*) ☐

**3** The sentences below describe the method which Ma and Pa used to stop the fire from getting near their house. Put the sentences in the correct order. e) has been done for you.

☐ a) Start a small fire on one side of the furrow.

☐ b) When the big fire gets near the furrow, there will be nothing left to catch fire.

☐ c) Make a furrow when the fire is still far away.

☐ d) Hit the small fire with something wet.

5 e) Then everything on that side of the furrow will burn.

☐ f) In this way the small fire will stay on the one side of the furrow.

**What do you think?**

1 What do you think happens next in the story?
2 What picture does the writer give you by using many sound and movement words?
3 What would you have done in this situation?
4 Do people today still put fires out in the way described in this story?
5 Have you ever been in a fire, or have you ever seen a fire? How did it start? Who put the fire out? How did they put it out?

**Vocabulary focus**

*k*

Pa **set** fire to the grass     . . .the sun had **set**

The same word in English can have several different meanings.

**1** Read the sentences and definitions below. Match each word in *italics* with the correct definition below. Write the correct letter of the sentence in each box. Look at numbers 1 and 2 as examples.

a) The police are sure that someone *set* fire to the house.
b) The sun rises in the east and *sets* in the west.
c) The bag is very *heavy*. I can't carry it.
d) He is a *heavy* smoker. He smokes a packet of cigarettes a day.
e) I'm afraid your dog can't come in the shop. *Tie* it up outside.
f) The two football clubs *tied* for first place. They both won all their matches this year.

60

g) Always make sure there are no cars coming before you *cross* the road.

h) If both of you do not stop talking and go to sleep, I will be very *cross*.

i) The child *beat* the dog with a piece of wood, and we never saw it again.

j) Argentina *beat* West Germany in the 1986 World Cup.

1 [j] to do better than

2 [i] to hit again and again

3 [ ] angry

4 [ ] to go from one side to the other

5 [ ] to go down in the sky

6 [ ] to make something burn

7 [ ] to be equal in a game

8 [ ] to use a piece of rope to keep something in the same place

9 [ ] a large amount

10 [ ] weighing a lot

**Grammar focus**

| Baby Carrie **was playing** on the floor |

We use the past progressive form (*was/were* + *verb-ing*) when we talk about an action over a period of time in the past. Something else often happens during this activity.

fire started
↓ ---------

Carrie was playing

*K*

*1* Make sentences about the activities of the different people in the story before the fire started. Look at number 1 as an example.

COLUMN *A*          COLUMN *B*

Ma                  work in the field
Carrie              study
Laura and Mary      cook
Pa                  play on the floor

1 Ma was cooking _____

2 _____

3 _____

4 _____

*2* Answer the questions truthfully.

1 Do you live alone or with someone? If you live with someone, what were you doing when he or she came home yesterday? _____

2 Have you visited anyone in the past few weeks? If you have, what was he or she doing when you arrived? _____

**Writing task**

Describe what you think happened next in the story. Say:
- if Ma and Pa were able to put the fire out
- if the fire reached the house
- if anyone was hurt
- if there was a lot of damage to the farm
- what the family did afterwards

# Why Me, I Kept Asking

**What about you?**

Millions of dollars collected
for the hungry of Africa

Emergency shipments of food sent
for the hungry of Ethiopia

**Famine in Ethiopia
Thousands near death**

## Children without food

1 What is the subject of these newspaper headlines?
2 Does the problem still exist?
3 What have people around the world done to help?

**Before you read**

Answer these questions.
1 Look at the pictures on the next page. How are they related to each other?
2 What do you think the text is about?
3 Write down five words you expect to read in the text.

_____    _____    _____    _____    _____

**Read the text**

Read the text on the opposite page. Does the text contain the words which you
wrote down?

**Check your understanding**

*1* Write down the number of the paragraph.

1 Which paragraph describes the feelings about the report?  ☐

2 Which paragraph describes what Geldof thought about after the report? ☐

3 Which paragraph describes what was in the news report?  ☐

*2* Fill in the blanks with words from the text. Write one word in each blank.

1 Geldof said that the problem was very, very big. He used the word

_____ . (*paragraph 1*)

2 Geldof said that the men, women and children did not look like people from

earth. He used the words _____ _____ _____ _____ .
(*paragraph 1*)

3 The reporter's voice showed that he did not know what to do about the

situation. The situation also made the reporter feel very sad, and it was very

bad to look at. Geldof said the reporter felt _____ , _____ and

_____ . (*paragraph 2*)

4 Geldof said that he would make a record and give the money to Oxfam. The

word which he used for the money which he would earn was _____ .
(*paragraph 3*)

5 Geldof said that he would show that he could not accept this situation. He

said he would _____ .(*paragraph 3*)

# Why me, I kept asking

The news report that night was about a famine in Ethiopia. From the first seconds it was clear that this was a really monumental catastrophe. The pictures were of people who
5 were so thin that they looked like beings from another planet. The camera focused on one man so that he looked directly at me, sitting in my comfortable living room. All around was the sound of death.

10 It was clear that somehow the world had not noticed this tragedy until now. You could hear the despair, grief and disgust in the voice of the reporter, Michael Buerk. At the end of the report he was silent. Paula started crying, then
15 rushed upstairs to check our baby, Fifi, who was sleeping peacefully.

I kept seeing the news pictures in my mind. What could I do? I was only a pop singer – and by now not a very successful pop singer. All I could do was make records which no one bought. But I would do that, I
20 would give all the profits of the next Rats[1] record to Oxfam[2]. What good would that do? It would only be a little money but it was more than I could give just from my bank account. Maybe some people would buy it because the profits were for Oxfam. And I would be protesting about
25 this disaster. But that was not enough.

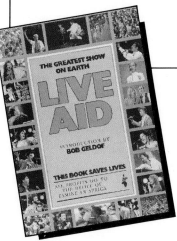

[1]*Rats*: the name of Bob Geldof's music group
[2]*Oxfam*: an organisation in Great Britain which helps poor people around the world

**3** What do you learn about Bob Geldof from the text? Put a tick ($\checkmark$) in the correct boxes.

1  He saw a news report on TV about the famine in Ethiopia. After the programme, he decided he had to do something about the problem. ☐

2  Bob Geldof and his wife felt very bad after seeing the report. ☐

3  His wife gave him ideas about how to help. ☐

4  He felt really bad because his life was easy compared to the people in the report. ☐

5  Bob Geldof was a pop singer at the time he saw the news report, but he was not making much money. ☐

6  Bob Geldof knew many other people who wanted to help. ☐

7  His ideas on how to collect money for the people in Ethiopia were very successful. ☐

8  Bob Geldof wanted to do more than just make a record. ☐

**What do you think?**

1  Have you seen any reports about famine on TV? Did you do anything about it?
2  Bob Geldof became famous for raising money for Africa. He organised events with other famous people. Do you think events such as Band Aid, Live Aid and Sport Aid are a good idea? Why?/Why not?

**Vocabulary focus**

| The baby was sleeping **peacefully**.    I wasn't a very **successful** pop singer. |

The suffix *-ful* is a common adjective ending. It has the general meaning of *full of* or *filled with*.

**1** Fill in each blank with one of the adjectives listed below.

colourful    hopeful    thoughtful
harmful    peaceful    useful

1  If something can help you, then it is _____ .
2  Something that may be dangerous to your health is _____ .
3  Someone who thinks about the feelings of other people is _____ .
4  If you have hope that something good will happen, then you are _____ .
5  A bird which has many colours is _____ .
6  A quiet day is a _____ one.

> The reporter **said,** 'The situation **is** terrible.'
> The reporter **said that** the situation **was** terrible.

When reporting what someone said in the past, the form of the verb usually changes. Look at the box below.

| | |
|---|---|
| 'I *work* for Oxfam,' he said.<br>He said (that) he *worked* for Oxfam. | *work → worked* |
| 'We *can* do something,' they said.<br>They said (that) they *could* do something. | *can → could* |

**1** In the third paragraph on page 63 Bob Geldof talks about his thoughts after the news report. Imagine that he had the same conversation with a friend. Fill in each blank in the conversation. Remember that Geldof is talking directly to a friend so you must change the form of the verbs. Look at the example.

**Geldof:** What __can__ __I__ __do__ ? I __am__ only a pop singer.

**Friend:** You can still help.

**Geldof:** All I ____ ____ ____ make records which no one ____ . But I ____ ____ that.

**Friend:** What do you mean?

**Geldof:** I ____ ____ all the profits of the next Rats record to Oxfam. Oh, but what good ____ ____ ____ ?

**Friend:** It sounds like a good idea to me.

**Geldof:** It ____ only ____ a little money but it ____ more than I ____ ____ just from my bank account.

**Friend:** That's for sure.

**Writing task**

Imagine that you want to do something to help the poor and hungry. Write a letter to Oxfam. You could include:
- how much you're enclosing
- what you or your government could do to help
Begin your letter like this:

your address
your city and postal code
today's date

Oxfam
Head Office
274 Banbury Road
Oxford

Dear Sir or Madam,

I am writing to you because I would like to do something to help people who are poor and hungry.

# About Lasers

**What about you?**

In this unit you are going to read about lasers. How much do you know about lasers? Put a tick (✓) next to the statements which are correct. Put a question mark (?) if you do not know the answer.

1 ☐ Lasers are a kind of light.

2 ☐ All light moves in waves.

3 ☐ Each beam of light has many light waves.

4 ☐ The light we see all around us is light of many different colours.

*Waves*

*A beam of light*

**Before you read**

The two texts you are going to read are called *About Lasers* and *How lasers make holes*. Read the five sentences from the texts below.

a) If the sentence describes lasers, write *About lasers* in the blank.

b) If the sentence describes how lasers make holes, write *How lasers make holes* in the blank.

1 Laser beams carry phone calls and TV pictures over long distances and play video discs. _____

2 Metals begin to heat rapidly now. _____

3 A laser beam is light of only one colour. _____

4 (Laser light) is just light but is quite different from ordinary light in several ways. _____

5 Almost immediately, the melted material gets so hot it boils away. _____

**Read the text**

Read the texts. Did you predict which texts the sentences were from?

---

# About lasers

A laser is a device which produces beams of a special kind of light – laser light. A
5 laser beam looks like a straight, almost solid, yet transparent[1] rod[2] of intense light. It is just light, but is quite different from ordinary light in several ways.
10 A laser beam is light of only one colour; ordinary 'white' light is many colours mixed together. Ordinary light spreads out in all directions;
15 laser beams stay almost parallel. The lightwaves in a laser beam are in step[3] with each other and work together to make the beam concentrated
20 and very bright; ordinary light waves are not in step[3]. In fact laser light is the brightest, most intense light known – even brighter than the sun.
25 Lasers are used to make all kinds of things from cars to clothing, from microchips to newspapers. Laser beams carry phone calls and TV
30 pictures over long distances and play video discs. Doctors also use lasers for 'bloodless surgery' which is less painful for the patient and easier for
35 the surgeon. The laser has often proved to be better than traditional methods in all of these jobs, and many more.

---

[1]*transparent*: can be seen through

[2]*rod*:

[3]

*waves in step*:

*waves not in step*:

---

# How lasers make holes

The focused[4] beam heats the surface of the material. Shiny things like metals reflect[5] much of the beam at first, so they heat the most slowly.
The surface starts to melt.

Shiny surface reflects light

Laser beam

Metals begin to heat rapidly now as the surface is dulled[6] by melting and there is less reflection.

Melting

Metal absorbs beam and heats rapidly

Almost immediately, the melted material gets so hot it boils away – vaporises. The beam goes in deeper, making a clean hole.

Melted material vaporizes

Laser makes clean hole

40

45

50

[4]*focused*: the meeting of beams of light on one point
[5]*reflect*: to throw back light
[6]*is dulled*: is made less shiny

**Check your understanding**

*1* In scientific writing it is easy to confuse noun phrases with verbs. This makes the text more difficult to understand. Read *How lasers make holes* again and underline all the verbs. Look at the example:

*Example:* Laser beams <u>carry</u> phone calls and TV pictures over long distances and <u>play</u> video discs.

*2* In each blank write the correct lines from *About Lasers*. Look at number as an example.

Which lines:

1 compare laser light and ordinary light?     lines 10–21

2 describe what laser light looks like?     _____

3 give a definition of a laser?     _____

4 give examples of the many uses of lasers?     _____

**3** The partially-completed notes below are about the texts on lasers. Fill in the blanks to complete the notes. (Remember that when you make notes you do not write down sentences from the text. You only write down the important words. Look at the notes already written down as examples.

① _What?_ _____ _Device produces beams of special light._

② _Looks like?_ _____

③ _How different from ordinary light?_ _____

_____ Laser _____ _____ Ordinary _____

a) _____ a) _____

b) _beams almost parallel (=)_ b) _beams spread out in all_

c) _____ _directions (≤)_

c) _____

④ _How different from all other light?_ _Brightest light known_

⑤ _Many uses - examples:_ _____

a) _____ c) _____ e) _____ g) _____

b) _____ d) _____ f) _____ h) _____

⑥ _One use - making holes_ _____

_How the laser works_ _____

_Step One:_ _____

_(Shiny things like metal heat most slowly; reflect at first)_

_Step Two:_ _____

_(Metals heat rapidly now; less reflection)_

_Step Three:_ _____

_Step Four:_ _Beam gets deeper making clean hole_

**What do you think?**

1 Have you ever seen a laser? What did it look like? What was it used for?
2 Do you know of any other uses of lasers? What are they?

| ordinary light spreads out | laser beams |
| a special kind of light | almost immediately |

In English the same letter(s) can have different pronunciations. For example:
a)  the *ea* sound in *beam* sounds like *see*
b)  the *ea* sound in *spread* sounds like *bed*

*1* Put each word below in the correct column. Look at the examples.

| beam | each | immediately | metal | spread |
| bread | even | intense | method | we |
| dead | heat | material | special | |

| /e/ – THE SOUND OF BED | | /i:/ – THE SOUND OF SEE | |
| --- | --- | --- | --- |
| E | EA | E | EA |
| special | spread | immediately | beam |

A laser is a device **which produces beams of a special kind of light**.

The sentence above gives a definition of a laser.

*1* Give definitions of the items in Column A. Write the correct sentence in each blank. Look at number 1 as an example.

| COLUMN **A** | COLUMN **B** |
| --- | --- |
| A laser | produces light. |
| A lamp | helps people see. |
| A pair of glasses | produces beams of a special kind of light. |
| A telephone | does mathematical problems. |
| A calculator | carries voices over long distances. |

1  <u>A laser is a device which produces beams of a special kind of light.</u>

2 _____

3 _____

4 _____

5 _____

Write a description of one of the uses of lasers which you know about. For example, you may wish to write about the use of lasers at pop concerts or in hospitals. Say:
  • what the laser is used for in this situation
  • what it looks like
  • what makes it so effective and/or interesting

Begin like this:
Lasers are used at/in . . .

# UNIT 16  Clothes Control

**What about you?**

1  Do you think a person's appearance is important? Why?/Why not?
2  What sort of clothes do you wear to school or to work?
   to parties, festivals or celebrations?
   around the house?
3  What are the advantages and disadvantages of uniforms?

**Before you read**  *K*  **1** Look at the pictures below. Then answer the questions. Give your reasons.

a)

c)

b)

1  Who is a traffic warden? ___b___
2  Who is a student nurse? ___a___
3  Who works in a supermarket? ___c___

**2** Now look at the pictures on the opposite page. They are pictures of the same people at work. Did you guess the people's occupations?

**Read the text**

The people in the pictures discuss their feelings about clothes. Read the texts quickly. Write the correct name under each picture at the end of the article. (Time limit: 1 minute)

# CLOTHES CONTROL

**Photos & interviews/Monica Wells**

Do your workclothes influence[1] the things you do and say? Do you change your personality[2] to match the clothes you're wearing at the time?

5     Asking these questions, we found that some rebel[3] against uniforms while others enjoy the change of clothes – and behaviour. . .!

### Madge Ramasar, 20

'The great thing about
10 wearing a uniform for work is that it stops competition between people with everyone trying to look better than
15 everyone else. On the practical side it stops my own clothes from getting worn and dirty. I don't really find any
20 disadvantages; people don't treat me differently just because I'm wearing a supermarket uniform.

'Wearing a uniform
25 also means I have more to choose from when I want something to wear out of work. I like to look smart and fashionable,
30 and really dress up if I go to a disco or party.'

### Arlene Earnshaw, 22

'A nurse's uniform goes with an expected kind of behaviour. On the
35 hospital ward, patients want to feel reassured, so once I put on the uniform, people expect me to be able to do
40 everything and to do it well with no problems of my own. I often have to hide my own feelings behind my uniform and
45 keep on smiling – the patient must come first.

'Outside the hospital, I like to look different from everyone else –
50 something I can't do at work! I design and make my own clothes – I make the most of showing who I am through my own
55 designer 'uniform'[4].'

### John St Aimee, 21

'Friends often don't recognise me in my uniform. If they do, they tease me and ask why
60 I'm behaving strangely. I think my uniform does take over[5] to a certain extent – you immediately get this feeling of being
65 better. I know I'm more serious at work.

'Outside work, I like to wear clothes I can relax in and be myself in; I'm
70 always larking around[6]. People often say traffic wardens are unfriendly, and I think they are surprised when we smile
75 at them!

'I used to hate wearing a uniform at school, but now I'm getting paid to wear one!'

[1] *influence*: to change what happens
[2] *personality*: a person's character
[3] *rebel*: to fight against something, often an idea
[4] *I make the most . . . designer 'uniform'*: by designing and making my own clothes, I can show who I really am
[5] *take over*: take control over
[6] *larking around*: making jokes, doing silly things

1 Name _____     2 Name _____     3 Name _____

**Check your understanding**

**1** Are these people *for* or *against* wearing uniforms? Read the statements below. If the statement is for wearing uniforms, write *for* in the blank. If the statement is against wearing uniforms, write *against* in the blank.

1 . . . it stops my own clothes from getting worn and dirty. _____

2 . . . I have more to choose from when I want something to wear out of work. _____

3 I often have to hide my own feelings behind my uniform and keep on smiling. . . _____

4 I used to hate wearing a uniform at school, but now I'm getting paid to wear one. _____

**2** How did Arlene, Madge and John answer the questions in the chart? Put a tick ( √ ) in the correct boxes if their answer is yes. Look at number 1 as an example.

| | ARLENE | MADGE | JOHN |
|---|---|---|---|
| 1 Do you act differently when you are in your workclothes? | √ | | √ |
| 2 Do you change your personality to match the clothes you're wearing at the time? | | | |
| 3 Do you like wearing a uniform? | | | |
| 4 Do you like wearing different clothes at work and out of work? | | | |
| 5 Do people treat you differently because you are a wearing a uniform? | | | |

**What do you think?**

1 Whom do you agree with – Arlene, Madge or John?
2 How do you feel when you wear a uniform or jeans? Do you feel differently in old clothes than you do in a suit or nice dress?
3 How do people in a uniform make you feel? For example, do you feel safe when you see a policeman or do you feel afraid?

**Vocabulary focus**

**1** Put these articles of clothing in appropriate boxes at the top of the next page. You can put some articles of clothing in more than one box.

| | | | |
|---|---|---|---|
| anorak | long-sleeved shirt | shoes | sweatshirt |
| blouse | nightdress | shorts | swimsuit |
| boots | overcoat | short-sleeved shirt | tights |
| cardigan | pullover | skirt | tie |
| dress | pyjamas | sleeveless dress | tracksuit |
| dressing gown | raincoat | slippers | trainers |
| gloves | sandals | socks | trousers |
| jacket | scarf | sweater | T-shirt |

| THINGS WOMEN WEAR | THINGS MEN WEAR |
|---|---|
|  |  |
| THINGS PEOPLE WEAR WHEN IT'S COLD | THINGS PEOPLE WEAR WHEN IT'S HOT |
|  |  |
| THINGS PEOPLE WEAR AT WORK OR SCHOOL | THINGS PEOPLE WEAR AT HOME |
|  |  |

**Grammar focus**

I make the most **of showing** who I am. . .
The great thing **about wearing** a uniform is that it stops competition. . .

Notice the verb form which we use after prepositions.

| PREPOSITION | GERUND (VERB + ING) |
|---|---|
| of | showing |
| about | wearing |

**1** Complete the sentences using your own ideas. Make sure you use gerunds in your answers.

1 I'm sorry for _____

2 I'm interested in _____

3 I'm thinking about _____

4 I'm tired of _____

5 I'm good at _____

**Writing task**

Imagine that a magazine has asked you to describe your feelings about the clothes you wear. Say:
- what you wear to school or to work
- how you feel in these clothes
- what you wear in your free time
- if you feel differently in these clothes

Begin like this:
When I am at _____ , I wear. . . .

# Answer key

## UNIT 1

### Check your understanding
**1** 1 dumb    2 smack   3 awful
    4 fantastic   5 super   6 notice
**2** 1 how old; Twenty-one; cannot be; twenty-two
    2 exams; worries; taking exams/taking them
    3 bed; awful; fantastic
**3** 1 Robert   2 Simon   3 Billy     4 Tanya
    5 Richard   6 Susan   7 Nicholas   8 Mark

### Vocabulary focus
**1 Make**: dinner; a mistake; money; a paper
aeroplane; a promise
**Do**: exercises; someone a favour; a good job;
homework; housework

### Grammar focus
**1** 1 Do you know where she lives?
    2 I asked her why she was late.
    3 I don't know how it happened.
    4 Does she know how much it costs?
**2** 1 ✓             5 ✓
    2 × – what I bought    6 × – why Barbara is
    3 × – this costs       unhappy
    4 × – time it is       7 ✓

## UNIT 2

### Check your understanding
**1** 1 c  2 a  3 b  4 a
    5 a  6 c  7 c  8 a
**2 Name**: Robert Cook **Other name**: Linen Cook
**Country**: Ireland **Occupation**: farmer **Year of
death**: 1726 **What he preferred**: white linen
clothes; white horses; vegetables; water
horses; vegetables; water
**3** 1, 2, 3 and 5 are correct.

### Vocabulary focus
**1** 1 not lucky  2 not important  3 not necessary
    4 not able
**2** 1 unpleasant  2 unkind  3 unhappy
    4 unhealthy
**3** 1 unable  2 unlucky  3 unhappy  4 unhealthy
    5 unnecessary

### Grammar focus
**1** 1 c  2 d  3 e  4 a  5 b

## UNIT 3

### Check your understanding
**1** 1 yes; no; yes; a      5 bad; bad dreams
    2 went near; went near  6 hole
    3 yes; he touched him   7 to have get well
      lightly; b             cards and presents
    4 no; no; yes; move a little   all around
**2** 1 c  2 a  3 d  4 b

### Vocabulary focus
**1** 1 thirty-four-year-old  4 five-mile
    2 four-hour            5 two-kilo
    3 six-month-old     6 ten-pound

### Grammar focus
**1**

**2**

| Verb | Past | Past Participle |
| --- | --- | --- |
| bend | bent | bent |
| fall | fell | fallen |
| fly | flew | flown |
| hold | held | held |
| keep | kept | kept |
| know | knew | known |
| lose | lost | lost |
| say | said | said |
| shake | shook | shaken |
| take | took | taken |
| tell | told | told |
| think | thought | thought |

## UNIT 4

### Before you read
1 There Are Some Men  2 Leonard Cohen
3 1934  4 Four
5 In each of the first three verses, there is one
sentence. In the fourth there are two sentences.

### Check your understanding
**1** 1 died  2 closed  3 stayed  4 sad  5 not
    6 sweet
**2** 1 c  2 d  3 a  4 b
**3** 1 and 4: Mountains are always there.
    2: People can see mountains from far away.
    3 and 5: Mountains are beautiful.

### Vocabulary focus
**1** 1 sea; see    2 hear; here  3 write; right
    4 knew; new  5 high; Hi

**2**

| Words | Meaning (Sample answers) |
| --- | --- |
| 1 morning | the early part of the day |
| 2 piece | a piece of cheese |
| 3 break | what happens to a glass if it falls |
| 4 allowed | when someone says you can do something |
| 5 dear | you being letters with this word |

# Answer key

## Grammar focus

**1** 1 Before  2 After  3 After  4 Before  5 never, sometimes, rarely, usually, often

**2** 1 × – I am never tired after I'swim.
2 √
3 × – Christopher rarely eats meat.
4 √
5 × – Have you always lived there?
6 × – They sometimes have pizza for dinner.

## UNIT 5

### Before you read

1 fat  2 moving them up and down  3 Keep Fidgeting classes  4 to lose weight, perhaps

### Read the text

**General word**: fidget  **Explanation**: nervous habit

### Check your understanding

**1** 1 however    2 significant  3 expend
4 researchers  5 heavy    6 slim
**2** 1 =  2 =  3 =  4 >  5 =  6 <

### Vocabulary focus

**1 thin**: slim, skinny, slender, underweight
**fat**: heavy, obese, plump, overweight
**2** 1 skinny  2 underweight  3 thin  4 slim
5 slender  6 plump  7 heavy  8 overweight
9 fat  10 obese

### Grammar focus

**1** (Sample Answers)
3 You should take exercise every day.
4 You shouldn't eat a lot of meat and eggs.
5 You should drink coffee without sugar.
6 You shouldn't eat biscuits.
7 You should eat fruit.

## UNIT 6

### Read the text

2 √  3 √  5 √

### Check your understanding

**1** 1 i  2 a  3 e  4 h  5 k  6 l  7 d  8 f  9 j
10 b

**2**

1. Pool depth 15 ft.  2. Board 20m high
3. Lots of men (50) in queue  4. Instructor looking cross
5. Instructor shouting, 'Jump!'
6. Last man saying, 'But I can't swim.'

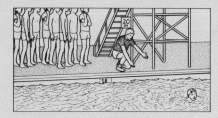

7. Instructor saying nothing  8. Swimmer floating

### Vocabulary focus

**1** 1 deep  2 long  3 high  4 wide
**2** 1 deepen; to make deeper
2 lengthen; to make longer
3 heighten; to make higher
4 widen; to make wider
5 shorten; to make shorter

### Grammar focus

**1** 1 × – Keep your legs straight when you kick.
2 √
3 √
4 × – Don't open your mouth when your head is in the water.
5 × – Move your arms when you move your legs.
6 × – Don't go swimming straight after lunch.

## UNIT 7

### Read the text

1 c  2 b  3 c  4 c  5 a

### Check your understanding

**1** 1 fool    2 parachute  3 raft    4 mad
5 souvenir  6 autograph  7 mourn
**2** 1 Lindbergh    2 $25,000    3 Lindbergh
4 office workers  5 Lindbergh's  6 clothes
7 cheques    8 America
**3** 2 ×  4 ×  6 ×

### Vocabulary focus

**Across**  2 rewrite  7 ton  9 remarry  11 on
12 hot  13 boy  15 refill  17 to  19 off  21 here
22 welcome
**Down**  1 prize  2 replay  3 we  4 it  5 to
6 engine  8 joy  9 reheat  10 rebuild  14 review
16 low  18 over  20 five

### Grammar focus

**1** (Sample answers)
1 angrily, badly, carefully, fast, happily, slowly, well
2 angrily, badly, carefully, fast, happily, quietly, slowly, well
3 angrily, fast, happily, quietly, slowly
4 angrily, carefully, hard, happily, quietly
5 hard

6 angrily, badly, carefully, easily, fast, happily, quietly, slowly, well
7 carefully, fast, happily, hard, slowly
8 angrily, happily, quietly
9 angrily, badly, carefully, easily, fast, happily, quietly, slowly, well
10 badly, carefully, fast, happily, hard, quietly, slowly, well

## UNIT 8

### Read the text
b) Why phonecards are good: c)
How you use a phonecard: a)
Where you can get a phonecard: b)

### Check your understanding
1  1 one=coin
   2 it=Phonecard
   3 them=Phonecards
   4 one=Phonecard
   5 They=Phonecard phoneboxes
   6 that=broken
   7 they=payphones
   8 one=Phonecard phone
   9 it=Phonecard

2 **How you use it:**
1 Go to a telephone box marked 'Phonecard'.
2 Put in your Phonecard.
3 Make your call.
4 Look at the screen to find out how many calls you can still make.
**How much it costs:**
One unit=10 p; 20 units=£2; 40 units=£4; 100 units=£10; 200 units=£20
**Why you should have a Phonecard:**
coins; vandalised
3  1 b  2 d  3 e  4 c

### Vocabulary focus
1 paper/clip  finger/nail  phone/card  hair/clip
hair/dryer  rain/coat  face/cloth  card/phone
card/phones  head/phones
2  1 raincoat  2 phonecard  3 hairdryer
4 headphones  5 cardphone

### Grammar focus
1  1 I'd like the striped ones./I'd like the ones with stripes.
   2 I'd like the round-necked one./I'd like the one with a round neck.
   3 I'd like the short ones.
2 (Sample Answers)
1 the blue ones
2 the small one
3 the brown ones, the black ones
4 No, I'm going to see the one with. . . . .

## UNIT 9

### Check your understanding
1 b 3  c 1  d 4  e 2
2  1 initials  2 distinguish  3 convince
4 identity  5 blankets  6 embarrassed

3  1 d  2 f  3 i  4 a  5 h  6 k  7 g  8 e  9·l
10 c  11 j  12 b
### Vocabulary focus
1  1 c  2 f  3 e  4 d  5 b  6 a

## UNIT 10

### Read the text
All the statements are false.

### Check your understanding
1  1 d  2 f  3 g  4 j  5 h  6 b  7 e  8 a
2 a) Home Baths 4%
  b) coastal 30%
  c) 120
  d) 101
  e) 19
3 1, 3, 4, 6 and 7, are connected to the information in the article.

### Vocabulary focus
1  2 accidental; accidentally
   3 danger; dangerously
   4 die
   5 difficult
   6 explanation
   7 prevent
   8 protection
   9 reality; realistically
   10 save; safe; safely
   11 warm; warmth; warmly
2  1 deaths  2 accidentally  3 warmed
   4 difficulty  5 prevent

### Grammar focus

| 1 | | | |
|---|---|---|---|
| bigger than | easier than | more common | worse than |
| colder than | healthier | than | better |
| higher than | than | than | than |
| safer than | prettier | more dangerous | |
| warmer than | than | than | |
| younger than | | more different than | |
| | | more isolated than | |
| the biggest | the easiest | the most common | the worst |
| the coldest | the healthiest | | the best |
| the highest | the | the most dangerous | |
| the safest | the prettiest | | |
| the warmest | | the most different | |
| the youngest | | the most isolated | |

# Answer key

**2** (Sample Answers)
1 warmer than  2 the most dangerous  3 safer than  4 The worst  5 the best  6 better than  7 easier than

## UNIT 11

### Read the text
4 A bank

### Check your understanding
**1** 1 b  2 a  3 a  4 b  5 b
**2** 1 Stoke
2 He was always broke.
3 An 'On Line' account.
4 He's a different bloke.
**3** £5; £3; yes
**4** 1 c  2 a  4 b

### Vocabulary focus
**1** 1 note      2 coin          3 change
4 cheque  5 credit card  6 cash

### Grammar focus
**1** 1 C  2 U  3 U  4 U  5 U  6 U  7 U  8 U
9 U  10 U  11 C  12 U  13 C  14 U
**3** 1 is      2 are; is  3 isn't    4 is
5 is    6 is        7 is/isn't  8 are

## UNIT 12

### Read the text
1 Question 2  2 Question 5  3 Question 4
4 Question 3  5 Question 7  6 Question 6
7 Question 1

### Check your understanding
**1** 1 b  2 b  3 a  4 b  5 a  6 b
**2** 1 f  2 d  3 a  4 c  5 h  6 g  7 i  8 b
**3** 1 . . . she eats a lot of hot food like soup
2 . . . sends her postcards from every place she visits
3 . . . she loves Spain even more
4 . . . because talking a lot is bad for her throat

### Vocabulary focus
**2** 1 flat        2 house  3 villa        4 palace
5 mansion  6 castle  7 block of flats
**3** (Sample Answers)
1 a strongly-built building or group of buildings; built in former times to defend against attack
2 a large building with many flats
3 built for people to live in; a group of rooms in a larger building
4 built for people to live in; usually more than one level
5 very large; usually for rich people
6 very large; for a king or queen
7 in the country; often used for holidays; usually with a garden

### Grammar focus
**1** 1 everything              6 anything
2 Somebody/Someone    7 something
3 anybody/anyone        8 anywhere
4 nothing
5 Everybody/Everyone

## UNIT 13

### Before you read
**Parents**: Pa, Ma
**Children**: Laura, Mary, Carrie
**Animals**: Jack, Bunny, Pet, Patty

### Check your understanding
**1** Number 3
**2** **Sound words**: shout, scream, roar, squeal, crackle
**Movement words**: rise, fly, run, hop, ripple, whirl, jerk, quiver, rush, climb
**3** 1 c  2 a  3 d  4 f  5 e  6 b

### Vocabulary focus
**1** 3 h  4 g  5 b  6 a  7 f  8 e  9 d  10 c

### Grammar focus
**1** 2 Carrie was playing on the floor.
3 Laura and Mary were studying.
4 Pa was working in the field

## UNIT 14

### Check your understanding
**1** 1 Paragraph 2  2 Paragraph 3  3 Paragraph 1
**2** 1 monumental              4 profits
2 beings from another planet  5 protest
3 despair, grief and disgust
**3** 1, 2, 4, 5, and 8 are correct.

### Vocabulary focus
**1** 1 useful    2 harmful    3 thoughtful
4 hopeful  5 colourful  6 peaceful

### Grammar focus
**1** What can I do? I am only a pop singer.
All I can do is make records which no one buys.
But I will do that.
I will give all the profits of the next Rats record to Oxfam. Oh, but what good will that do?
It will only be a little money but it is more than I can give just from my bank account.

## UNIT 15

### What about you?
All the statements are true.

### Read the text
1, 3 and 4 are from *About Lasers*
2 and 5 are from *How lasers make holes*

## Check your understanding

1 heats; reflect; heat; starts to melt; begin to heat; is dulled; is; gets; boils; vaporises; goes

2 2 lines 4–7   3 lines 1–4   4 lines 25–35

3 2 straight, almost solid, yet transparent rod intense light

   3 a) one colour; many colours
      c) in step; not in step

   5 a) cars        b) clothing    c) microchips
      d) newspapers e) phone calls  f) TV pictures
      g) video discs  h) surgery

   6 Step One: Focused beam heats surface material
      Step Two: Surface starts melt
      Step Three: Melted material vaporises

## Vocabulary focus

1 /e/:   e– special, method, intense, metal
          ea– spread, bread, dead

  /iː/   e– immediately, even, material, we
          ea– beam, each, heat

## Grammar focus

1 1 A laser is a device which produces beams of a special kind of light.

  2 A lamp is a device which produces light.

  3 A pair of glasses is a device which helps people see.

  4 A telephone is a device which carries voices over long distances.

  5 A calculator is a device which does mathematical problems.

## UNIT 16

### Before you read

1 1 b  2 c  3 a

### Read the text

1 Madge Ramasar  2 Arlene Earnshaw
3 John St Aimee

## Check your understanding

1 1 for  2 for  3 against  4 for

2 1 Arlene; John  2 Arlene; John  3 Madge; John
  4 Arlene; Madge; John  5 Arlene; John

## Vocabulary focus

1 (Sample Answers)

| | |
|---|---|
| Things women wear | – everything but a tie |
| Things men wear | – everything but blouse, dress, nightdress, skirt, sleeveless dress, tights |
| When it's cold | – anorak, boots, cardigan, dressing gown, gloves, overcoat, pullover, scarf, sweater, sweatshirt, tights |
| When it's hot | – sandals, shorts, short-sleeved shirt, sleeveless dress, swimsuit |
| At work or school | – everything but anorak, dressing gown, gloves, nightdress, overcoat, pyjamas, raincoat, slippers, swimsuit |
| At home | – **everything but anorak, overcoat, raincoat, swimsuit** |

## Grammar focus

1 (Sample Answers)

  1 I'm sorry for not being on time.

  2 I'm interested in learning how to ski.

  3 I'm thinking about going to the sea on holiday.

  4 I'm tired of studying hard.

  5 I'm good at swimming.